BLACK COP

MY 36 YEARS IN POLICE WORK, AND MY CAREER-ENDING EXPERIENCES WITH OFFICIAL RACISM

CALVIN LAWRENCE
WITH MILES HOWE

James Lorimer & Company Ltd., Publishers
Toronto

James Lorimer & Company Ltd., Publishers acknowledges funding support from the Ontario Arts Council (OAC), an agency of the Government of Ontario. We acknowledge the support of the Canada Council for the Arts, which last year invested $153 million to bring the arts to Canadians throughout the country. This project has been made possible in part by the Government of Canada and with the support of Ontario Creates.

Cover design: Tyler Cleroux
Cover images: Calvin Lawrence
Photo of Miles Howe: Barbra Lalonde

Library and Archives Canada Cataloguing in Publication

Title: Black cop : my 36 years in police work, and my career-ending experiences with official racism / Calvin Lawrence with Miles Howe.

Names: Lawrence, Calvin, 1949- author. | Howe, Miles, 1977- author.

Description: Includes index. Identifiers: Canadiana (print) 20190142871 | Canadiana (ebook) 20190142898 | ISBN 9781459414488 (softcover) | ISBN 9781459414495 (epub)

Subjects: LCSH: Lawrence, Calvin, 1949- | LCSH: Police—Canada—Biography. | LCSH: Racism—Canada—Case studies. | LCGFT: Autobiographies. | LCGFT: Case studies.

Classification: LCC HV7911.L386 A3 2019 | DDC 363.2092—dc23

James Lorimer & Company Ltd., Publishers
117 Peter Street, Suite 304
Toronto, ON, Canada
M5V 0M3
www.lorimer.ca

Printed and bound in Canada.

CONTENTS

Black and white people should read this book.
It's the story of justice and injustice in policing.
After reading it, I can't tell you what side you should come
down on. I can only tell you that it is a black man's story.

There are many like it, but this one is mine.

CHAPTER 1
BLACK CONSCIOUSNESS

Some mornings I can deal with the pain. It's my knees more than any other body part that have stopped co-operating. I can't get them to bend anymore. Depending on the intensity of the ache when I open my eyes, I pull on one or both of my knee braces. I look over at my wife and give her a kiss while she sleeps. Then I go downstairs, or maybe downtown, into the sunrise chill. I let the motion come back, slowly, into my joints. I wrap my hands in fighter's tape, layer over layer, and start in on the punching bag.

Other mornings when I get up I feel like the seventy-year-old man that I am — limping stiff around the house in my slippers and bathrobe, carrying thirty pounds I could stand to lose, one hand on my back, standing there waiting for the fucking pills to kick in. Still wondering how I ever got to this point.

I will say that the anger has finally subsided. I got big. I turned my fists into lethal weapons. I carry at least one knife on my person, usually some kind of special blade, something to cut through seatbelt webbing and shatter car windows. I've got a room at home filled with special-order weapons from the army surplus store. The weapons excite me, and the desire to stay armed — to stay prepared for the potential attack I know might come at any time — is real for me. But I don't worry that I'm a danger to those around me anymore, or that I might go off on a revenge fantasy and kill a bunch of my ex-co-workers. I'm not going to "lose control." So you can relax.

Every time I'm followed while shopping, every time I'm spoken down to — I don't accept it, but I have come to understand it. I don't have any more unanswered questions or self-doubt, and I no longer blame myself. I understand the system that I was born into and that I will die out of. I am a victim of and a participant in that system. But it isn't my doing or my fault.

I tried.

I'm a retired black cop. I won't apologize for that. And we can — and will — talk about what that means from a racial perspective. I am from a time when cops walked the neighbourhoods at night with our toes freezing, jostling doorknobs, crouching down in alleyways in the shadows behind dumpsters and trash cans, with fish heads and grease buckets and broken bottles. And I am from the generation that watched our mothers clean houses and our fathers make bunks on railcars and say "Yes, sir," and "No, ma'am." To be a cop was a way to attain a level of prestige and advancement that was otherwise inaccessible to us.

I've sat in squad cars, at times in shape and at times out of shape, watching, drinking a fifth coffee, while each muscle begged me to move.

I've chased suspects in a flat-out run, and I predate the days of orthopedic inserts in police boots, predictive modelling software and YouTube training videos.

I've been punched, scratched, kicked and called everything but a man. And I wouldn't change a minute of it.

I was born on May 31, 1949, in Yarmouth, Nova Scotia, to Frieda and William Lawrence. I had four older sisters and two older brothers. I was a late child in a rocky marriage. Because of certain hardships, which aren't really your business, I was given up for adoption to my father's brother and his wife, who had no children. I'm sure in some way this has led to abandonment issues for me. Somebody wanted me . . . but somebody didn't. That's always the way it is.

As a child, I visited my birth parents here at 10 Haskell Street in Yarmouth, Nova Scotia.

I could tell you that there was family dysfunction. I could say that intergenerational trauma didn't allow my parents to make healthy decisions for the family. The history of racial abuse made everyone, including myself, hypervigilant. I'm satisfied with knowing what I know. Although I did call my aunt and uncle Mom and Dad, I know I was loved and nurtured by two sets of parents.

Through later conversations with my family, I came to realize that the circumstances of my childhood weren't unusual. All around me, kids were being raised by their grandparents, aunts, uncles and cousins. We simply could not afford — nor were we necessarily comfortable with — the nuclear family model, and in those days bringing a child up was more of a community affair. In my case, this meant that the seventh child in the house — the latecomer — was too much. So that kid — me — was given to my father's brother and his wife, who had none of their own. And we still all stayed close and visited whenever we could. Although this arrangement of intra-familial adoption might seem strange to you, it's not at all unusual to have extended family raise a child in the black community.

To paraphrase Dr. Frances Welsing from her book *The Isis Papers: The Keys to the Colors*, in a society dominated by white supremacist behaviour, it's impossible to have a "functional" black family. For Dr. Welsing, a family operating under these circumstances is less of a family and more of a "survival unit." Any family in which the members are regularly harassed, bullied, underemployed or unemployed is going to be off balance. If you're black, it doesn't matter what you did or what you do. If you're a black person, you are, from cradle to grave, the target of racist behaviour.

So what does dysfunctional mean, if, according to author

Calvin at four years old, with father, Colin Lawrence, in the backyard on Maynard Street in 1953.

John Bradshaw, I tell you that 97 per cent of our families are dysfunctional?

Was it my family situation that was dysfunctional?

Or was it the social demands placed on my family that were dysfunctional?

My father's brother Colin and his wife Mildred brought me from Yarmouth, on the sleepy west coast of Nova Scotia, to Halifax, the largest Canadian city east of Montreal. Colin was black. Mildred, my adoptive mother, was white. They loved each other deeply. In Halifax, their love was a source of interest for the racists, gossips, prudes, puritans, nosey neighbours and busybodies. And you hear a lot when you're playing outside the house in a neighbourhood where everyone knows — or aims to know — everyone else's business. We had a neighbour who, when hanging out her laundry, never tired of sucking her teeth and saying, "Hmm. He

Calvin at eight years old, in front of the family residence on Maynard Street in Halifax, Nova Scotia, in 1957.

shoulda' stuck with his own race. In mixed marriages, it's the children who suffer."

Have you heard that? That the children suffer in a mixed marriage? What do people mean when they say this? It means that these "mixed-up" children will suffer hardships because they're not white. Their black blood will follow them around like a curse, shutting the door on opportunities and potential. A black child will come to know their place. A white child will have the world. A mixed-marriage child will come to regret their lot.

There's a pecking order of skin colour among black people, taught to us as children in the playground. We'd beat out a rhythm to it, clapping, stomping, jumping rope to it as though it was common knowledge. Dr. Welsing is not wrong when she repeats one of our earliest childhood rhymes:

If you're Black, get back.
If you're Yellow, you're mellow.
If you're Brown, stick around.
If you're White, you're all right.

In Halifax, I grew up in a thriving, mixed black and white community around Gottingen Street. There were shops, a Metropolitan store, hardware stores, banks, a post office and lots of restaurants. From my knee-high perspective, it was a vibrant array of sights and sounds. I remember walking hand-in-hand with my father, meeting his friends, putting my tiny hand in theirs and saying, "how do you do?" Sometimes we'd go to the train station to pick up his paycheque. The thundering sounds of the big train engines stay with me to this day.

Calvin at home on Maynard Street with mother, Mildred Lawrence, and father, Colin Lawrence, in 1959.

On Saturdays, my father and I would take our fishing poles and get on the public bus, down to the South End to catch fish off the public wharf. We'd put what we caught — pollock, mackerel, whatever — into a brown leather bag and ride the bus home with our booty. We'd make the whole bus smell like a fishmonger's!

My mom was a homemaker. She was always there for me. She was the glue in our family. She was the buffer between me and my father when we had disagreements. She expected the best of me, and I tried to never disappoint her.

I suspect that, because she married a black man, she was ostracized by her family. She never talked about it. I never asked — I was too young to even formulate the question. But there was only ever sporadic contact between her and her family in Chezzetcook, Nova Scotia, an hour's drive from Halifax. Decades later, when she passed in her eighties,

I didn't even know of anyone from her birth family to notify of her death.

In the early sixties, when I was a child, there was no major crime in our neighbourhood. It was a self-contained — and self-monitoring — community. You'd see people drinking, and there were the bootleggers who brewed up moonshine in their basements, but that was the extent of it. I'd walk the streets without fear and greet the shopkeepers by name. It was as though people were more in tune with each other and content to socialize among themselves. On Saturday nights, some folks would sit on their front steps to chat and greet and catch up with the people passing by. Others would hang out on the street corners, chatting with each other, getting the latest news.

Learning to become a black man, I watched the black men around me. The men I saw dressed well — three-piece suits and vests, shined shoes and fedoras. Many of these men worked with my father on the railroad and comported them-selves with dignity. I saw everybody drink, too much once in a while, but it was done in somebody's house; they weren't falling down drunk on the street. The people I saw, for the most part, were people who had self-control. They got up and went to work in the morning, even if they were hung-over.

The black community in Halifax was tight-knit. Your parents worked with your friends' parents. Your parents knew your friends, and theirs knew you. If you did some-thing wrong out on the street, or in school, you could bet that word travelled faster than you, and that your mom and dad knew about it by the time you got home. If you acted out, you could expect that someone on the street would go out of their way to give you a verbal comeuppance. This was the way of the black community, and it spoke to the collective responsibilities and roles in raising its children. A child was a neighbourhood endeavour.

In the evenings, music would flow from black entertainment centres, places like the Arrows Club, the Gerrish Street Hall and Club Unusual. Our music and culture, for the most part, came up from the United States — the Temptations, the Supremes, Gladys Knight. There were the sounds of Motown and Chicago blues. We devoured black American culture and called it our own. On hot July and August nights, I'd keep the bedroom window propped open and stay up late, listening to the thumping bass.

When spring came and the cool breezes off the Atlantic brought the smells of seaweed and sea salt wafting through the house, it signalled that it was time to get a job. It was frowned on by the community to not be looking for work when school let out. I had a paper route and delivered pamphlets, door to door. I scrubbed floors for Modern Building and Cleaning for $1.10 an hour. And I went down to the South End and got on my hands and knees to pull weeds for the rich white folks in their mansions. There was always something to do, and I figured, at this young age, that nothing was going to get in my way.

The problem was, I was a kid. And I was seeing adults from my community all doing the same types of jobs. It was as though we had collectively resigned ourselves to it. We weren't investing in our own companies. And, for the most part, we weren't opening our own businesses. We would just head down to the South End, hat in hand, looking for menial labour jobs. We had watched our mothers and fathers do it, so we did it too. The years went by, and we lived with the hope that we would progress to bigger and better things in life. And as those dreams remained unfulfilled, bitterness

The Desegregation of Schools. Miss Johnston's 1955 Grade One Class, Joseph Howe School
Schools in Nova Scotia were formally desegregated only in 1954. But many schools had already desegregated. Miss Johnson's Grade One Class in Halifax's North End was one. Note Mr. Garfield Simmonds (far right, second row), now teaching at Joseph Howe. *shunpiking* has relied on the 50-year memory bank of Gregory States, David Holton and Claude Isaacs. So, if you can help us with the missing names, please call 455-4922. Front Row (L-R) — David Houghton, Marcia Barton, Jean Adams, Carole Streeter, Jean Poole, Linda Williams, Elaine Skinner, ?, Evelyn Meade, Roy Mah. Middle Row (L-R) — Audrey Riles, Terranie Publicover, Richard Smith, Gregory States, Maxine Browne, Charlene Oliver, Diane David, Phyllis Townsend, Sheila Lucas, Alexander Thomas, Calvin Lawrence, ?, Gregory Bauld, Garfield Simmonds. Back Row (L-R) — Claude Isaacs, Darrel Braithwaite, ?, Francis David, ?, Linda Strangward, Jerry Randall, Douglas Hickey, Wayne Croft, Ken Langille, Miss Johnson.

This news clipping recalls the desegregation of schools in Nova Scotia, using Calvin's grade one class at Joseph Howe School in 1955 as an example.

and frustration became an undertone in our community. As William Grier and Price Cobbs say in their book *The Jesus Bag*, the defining emotion of the black experience is anger. Lack of opportunity and racially motivated insults, whether covert or overt, were part of being an African Nova Scotian. We were expected to know our place and not strive to get ahead.

The era of hard drugs began in the late seventies, and the black community suffered. Everything changed, and not for the better. What economic prosperity our community had enjoyed disappeared. With few exceptions, most of the businesses on Gottingen Street shut their doors. New businesses opened up that extracted money from the community without reinvesting in it, its future or its infrastructure. Slowly, "For Sale" signs, boarded up shop windows and vacant houses became a common part of our landscape. Property values tanked. Real estate speculation, then gentrification inched its way into the community. Now, when I return to Gottingen Street in my own old age, next door to abandoned buildings there are pricey restaurants, boutiques and condo towers selling units for three hundred thousand dollars or more. Almost nothing is black-owned.

I predict that in the near future, Halifax developers will transform the last holdouts of the old black neighbourhoods, Uniacke Square and Brunswick Towers. In their place, we'll have boutique hotels and tapas bars we can't afford to stay in or eat at. And down the road? Other than from photographs and books, I don't think you'll ever even know that black people lived in the area.

Remember that the black community was concentrated in certain well-defined areas of Halifax. This was related both to poverty and to the understanding that there was safety in numbers. As a black person, there were areas of Halifax that were out of bounds to you. If you dared to venture into those areas, especially alone, white people would insult you and call you names. It didn't usually get to the point of physical confrontation, but the disrespect and hatred was palpable, especially when white people were in a group that affirmed and reinforced their behaviour.

When I was growing up, segregation was still legally "on the books" in Nova Scotia. I was aware of the segregated schools in other parts of the province, and I attended burials in segregated cemeteries. We also knew of the "sundown towns" — smaller, "whites only" towns and villages all across

Nova Scotia that didn't allow for blacks or First Nations people after dark. But for the most part, the segregation was covert, and the racism was refined.

For example, say you went to a nightclub downtown. In those days, they'd usually be playing black music. Soul music. Motown. If management saw a lot of black kids in the club, not doing anything out of order, just dancing, they'd change the playlist to country and western — so-called white music. Too many blacks in one place was considered to be trouble just waiting to happen.

On nights out with your buddies, you'd get checked for ID. Bouncers would stop you even when it was obvious you were old enough to be there. Staff would challenge you on what you were wearing, as if there were a dress code. You'd look inside the club and see white folks wearing the same thing you had on. Sometimes, black patrons would get frustrated and get into shouting matches with the doormen. But rarely did these confrontations become physical.

We'd usually just get the message and leave.

My first recollection of being discriminated against took place when I trying to make a little money at the Dominion Store near the corner of North and Agricola Streets. As little children, we'd line up outside the Dominion with our red wagons and offer to wheel groceries to customers' homes, for a few cents in tips. There were a bunch of us from different neighbourhoods, all young and proud, showing off our wagons. I was the only black kid in the group. A cop who was working on Agricola Street came into the parking lot, right up to me, right in front of the ·group, and told me, "You shouldn't be here. Go home. Get outta here."

He shooed me away with his hand, as if I was something undesirable, like a fly or a stray dog. I was just a kid. But when you're black in Nova Scotia, you learn young that racist behaviour doesn't have an age limit.

When I was thirteen, we moved from Maynard Street, which was in the heart of a mixed-race area, to Belle Aire Terrace, a predominantly white street. The move was supposed to be a step up on the social and economic ladder. But the racial composition of our little family did not go unnoticed on Belle Aire Terrace. We raised eyebrows and caused whispers in the new neighbourhood. Right away I had trouble with other youths, and, looking back, I can't imagine their parents didn't know what they were doing. There were a number of them who bullied me cruelly, and I can only attribute it to the fact that my black skin was understood as an invitation — a duty — to attack.

The verbal and physical attacks quickly became a pattern. I learned to fear leaving the house and would try to time my exits and entrances for the least chance of meeting up with the neighbourhood kids. I'd come home with bruises and scrapes or with tears streaming down my face, saddened over some racial insult whose meaning I didn't quite understand, but whose delivery and intent was clearly meant to harm.

My mother would ask whether the kids bullying me were white or black; I answered that I didn't know. As a kid, I didn't see it. I couldn't make that racial distinction in my mind. Maybe it was because my mom was white and my dad black. Maybe I was just a slow learner, or naïve. I don't know.

In our house, there was no talk of hating all white people, or of all white people being racists. We weren't that polarized, and we didn't generalize along those terms, and it never dawned on me that there was this tumultuous, generations-old, race-based conflict going on around us. Or that things were about ready to explode.

Many of the black youth in Halifax got taught their lessons quite early on, either by the cops or by their white neighbours. My dad was not a political activist, nor was my mom. He was more concerned with my safety as an individual and in keeping the family intact, as opposed to engaging in the struggle against racist behaviour or in the bigger picture of black rights.

I remember going to dances as a teenager at Saint Mark's Church. There'd be black kids and white kids, and there'd be dancing. And the dancing would be followed by fighting. One night, a black friend asked me, "How come you don't fight?"

I answered, "Why would I fight?"

He said, "For your colour!"

My awareness of being black and singled out — and being suspect — began when my father bought me a Honda two-stroke, 50cc motorcycle to ride to and from high school. It was a beautiful gift, and I loved riding through the streets on it. Police officers in Halifax would stop me frequently, and their attitude was, "Where did *you*, a black boy, get the money to buy *this*?" I'd tell them my father bought it for me, but it never ended there. They'd come back with, "*Where* does he work?"

These interactions created a sense of fear and apprehension in me whenever I kick-started my bike. It soured the whole experience, from a gift given in love to an object that caused me to pre-emptively cower against the police. Slowly, I came to understand that if, as a black person, you obtain what is supposedly reserved for white people — a motorcycle, a nice car or whatever — the police immediately suspect you of theft and criminality. You have to prove your innocence.

Nothing has changed. These days they've institutional-
ized the processes. We rally against "racial profiling," and
they just change its name to "risk analysis." Computerized
data points brand our neighbourhoods as "high crime," and
white security professionals make money writing supposedly
objective books on us and giving seminars on the subject of
black suffering at the hands of police.

And it was never any different.

We used to hang out on the street corners and talk. I
guess it's a cultural habit of black people to stand on corners.
Back in the day, it was better than the internet. It was where
we got our news. We had our two favourite corners —
Gerrish and Gottingen Street, and Gerrish and Creighton
Street. If we weren't on the corners, we'd be sitting on the
front steps at somebody's house, catching up.

"What's happening? What's going on? What's up?"

You'd think we were plotting the overthrow of white
society, given the way that some of the police acted. Halifax
police would come along and chase us away from the corners
and charge us with loitering if we didn't disperse. White
society always comes at us with this attitude of "They must
be planning something. Something *bad*."

If you dated a white girl, you had to drop her off around
the corner from her house. As youth, we would get a lot
of grief from the police if we were seen with a white girl.
Maybe the cops thought they were meant to protect the
virtue of these girls against us. Maybe they were just hoping
to pre-emptively save a future mixed-race baby from the
shame of life.

There were a couple of detectives who would patrol
around town. They took themselves to be quite important
and called themselves Vice. If these two saw you talking to a

white girl, they'd roast you. They'd come up on you with an aggressive attitude, all finger-waving in your face and snarling at you. They'd write your name up in their notebooks, like they were crafting up future criminals out of children.

There was none of this so-called "multicultural" environment. There was no sensitivity about it. It was black. And it was white. It was a "you stick with yours, and we'll stick with ours" attitude. This rule applied, except of course when white men would come prowling through the black community. Then, when these distinguished gentlemen were on the hunt for their supposedly "exotic" black women, who they considered "loose" and available, the cops turned a blind eye.

In the black community, the church was important on many levels. It was our place of meeting, our place of prayer and a symbol of our vitality. As a youth, I attended Cornwallis Street Baptist Church (now known as New Horizons Baptist Church), which was built in 1832 and still stands to this day. Gathering all together on Sundays in our finest was the norm, and even if my parents didn't go, they made sure that I attended. It was in this foundation that I learned the values of respect and community ethics. But religion alone was not going to give us equality in white society, and it was this that our spirits cried out for.

During my time at Cornwallis Street Baptist, a number of different ministers passed through. The person who had the biggest impact on me was Reverend Coleman, an American. He knew how to push back against racist behaviour, and he blended religion with the cry for equality. He wasn't afraid to get angry and aggressive about the racist behaviour that was hurting the black community. He'd challenge commercial establishments that prevented black people from entering or were harassing black clientele. Coleman had an American flair for pushing the envelope when it came to facing down racist behaviour. And he wasn't afraid to hold black people accountable for their own behaviours. If we were out of line, either as individuals or a community, he would express his displeasure from the pulpit.

But what about Africville?

The history of Africville wasn't taught in any schools — and mostly still isn't. It might have been mentioned, from time to time, in one of Coleman's sermons. But that was the sum total of it. I knew of Africville. But as a youth I didn't go there. My interactions with folks from Africville were limited to Bloomfield Junior High School, where I attended. Bloomfield was for the most part a white school with a few black students from Africville and a smattering of black youth from the mixed neighbourhoods. I'm still in touch with some of those people today.

To be clear, Africville and the Prestons were *the* black communities in the Greater Halifax area. For the most part, these were the segregated — blacks only — communities where the descendants of black settlements from the eighteenth and nineteenth centuries still lived and thrived.

Because of the historical precedence of self-reliance, there was a closed nature to some of the black communities in Nova Scotia. Some black communities did not really welcome outsiders. Other communities, while not closed, were wary of others, even other black people. I think some communities, if they didn't know you, suspected that you were there to exploit them. So even though I could trace my own black heritage back seven generations to the black Loyalists — to slaves fleeing persecution in upstate New York — I couldn't just wander into Africville or the Prestons and expect a royal welcome based upon a shared history and skin colour. We all might have had a certain common experience of being black in the Maritimes, but that experience didn't necessarily translate into good vibes. Each black community was unique.

Africville had a long and fabled history. It was a community unto itself, and to a degree was largely ignored by the larger white populace. It was the stronghold. There were backyard gardens. There were people who lived off the land, and there were skilled tradespeople who helped each other. Although Africville residents paid municipal taxes in Halifax, they were often denied basic municipal services such as garbage removal, water supply and sewers. Despite the city working to undermine it, Africville was an independent and resourceful community.

Africville fit into a similar, well-established pattern of underfunding black communities elsewhere in the province. Judging from the lack of political will or interest in improving these communities, I'd say this inequity was systemic and was not a problem unique to any one level or area of governance. After all, we were the easily identifiable "underclass." Why should we have sewers or clean drinking water or garbage removal, even though we paid taxes? We had no political power and were treated as powerless.

Africville was surrounded by toxic and harmful industries and businesses. These were the types of industries you would never want around your home. Anything that wasn't acceptable to the quality of life of Halifax's white community, they'd build around Africville. There was an abattoir, a tuberculosis hospital, a city dump and a prison at the end of Gottingen Street. These days, we call this "environmental racism."

The intention was to make Africville as inhospitable as

possible. But when the community wouldn't buckle under the lack of services and the toxic industries being placed all around it, the municipal government simply tired of kid-gloving the resistance to its plans. The city of Halifax expropriated Africville and razed the community to the ground.

And that's what kick-started this whole story.

The way the city of Halifax dealt with Africville was disgusting; it was shameful. They just brought bulldozers in and levelled garden patches, tore down clothes lines and took down homemade houses that had been passed down through the generations. By the mid-sixties, municipal workers had demolished the church — the heart and core of the Africville community. While people slept, bulldozers would ram into their houses. I've heard stories of elders who were in hospital, only to return to find their houses destroyed.

Municipal officials would traipse into Africville, flashing suitcases full of money around to entice black residents to relocate. The city used dump trucks to relocate households out of Africville. And after the expropriation, many families were forced into public housing projects such as Mulgrave Park and Uniacke Square. The Africville expropriation was devastating, literally and figuratively. It garnered national, then international attention. Hundreds of people had been forcibly displaced, and the black community's angry response flared in the streets.

My personal experience of the razing of Africville was delivered via a number of filters. At the time, I didn't understand the significant impact that this destruction had on the people involved. The city, typical of a deeply racist organization, claimed that what it had perpetrated was for the explicit good of its blacks — if only they could understand it.

When I heard statements from city officials, I didn't doubt their truth. For me, still young and unaware of geographical racism, it was all just a neutral process happening around me. My beatings on Belle Aire Terrace didn't transfer to a collective black experience. Our family conversations around the dinner table were focused on self-preservation against the flood waters that were beginning to rise all around us.

Prior to the turbulent sixties and the overflowing influence of what was occurring in the United States, most Nova Scotia blacks wishing to challenge the racist behaviour that was endemic to life utilized our well-established avenues of resistance. The black community would organize meetings with local politicians on issues related to human rights abuses. These might produce some type of movement on a particular, specific issue, but it was always done within the parameters of white society. The fundamental inequity of the system was never questioned. Racist behaviour was taken as an immovable object — a fact of life of being black. I remember one particular ad campaign called Give a Damn. This was a campaign meant to tug on the heartstrings of local white business owners. From time to time, we'd hear an advertisement over the radio saying, "Give a damn. Hire a black student."

Hat in hand.

The best we were supposed to expect was sympathy and handouts. For the most part, any challenges to the white power structure would only go as far as white society's comfort level. And remember, to the people in power who practice racist behaviour, equality feels like oppression.

But after 1967? After the expropriation of Africville? Then things changed for a while. The anger of the community spilled out of the confines of the church and out of the established avenues of accepted activism. Black conservative leaders could no longer control the anger and frustration of young people in the community. There was violence in streets. The regular "minor" episodes of racist behaviour that we had come to understand as being part of living in Halifax would now result in riots. I remember waking up and hearing on the news that a spark had ignited a riot after a function at the Halifax Forum. My parents didn't take a stand on it. Other than monitoring my comings and goings and having faith in what they'd taught me, they remained largely mute on the unrest. At least in front of me.

I was strictly an observer during the riots. To me it all happened so fast and was such a different experience. I didn't have time to form an opinion about what was going on. I didn't know who was right and who was wrong. So I didn't align with any side. I had led a sheltered and controlled life. As a result, I was neutral about the situations I was seeing. I was also still young enough to think I could accomplish anything I wanted to through hard work, and that I could navigate my way through the system. No one had ever told me otherwise.

I knew that racist behaviour happened. But I understood racism as a series of singular, unrelated incidents. There were always racial slurs levelled at me in school and in different areas of the city. But I assumed these were unique, disparate events. Today, looking back with a set of seventy-year-old eyes and a lifetime of experience behind me, I have felt the frustration, the anger and the helplessness, the hopelessness and confusion of being black while trying to succeed in white society.

If I had known then what I know now, would I have participated in the riots?

Still, my answer would be no.

For my parents' peace of mind, I would never have risked arrest and bringing shame on the Lawrence name. That being said, I fully understand the frustrations of today's black youth who have given up hope of pursuing mainstream avenues for success. And I can't say that I blame them when they try to wrestle away what white society will not permit them a chance to earn.

In the late '60s in Halifax, there were people in the black community, like Rocky Jones, who did not condone the violence, but who also did not oppose it. In response to the riots, he and others were saying, "Look, there's going to be more of this violence if we don't see change in relation to racist behaviour."

Rocky was perceived by many in the community as a new type of leader. He was a powerful presence. And other than my father and his brothers, I had never been exposed to people who modelled black male power on a level beyond the family and the community. Certainly, every day I saw black men who'd stand up for their families and stand up for themselves. But to go out and advocate for black progress by any means necessary? Violence included?

There weren't many who would do that.

We'd never seen this open, radical challenge coming from the black community towards the white government of Halifax. And this defiance of the status quo garnered Rocky many followers. Black people, long aware of their marginalized status, became radicalized and politicized. They weren't going to accept it anymore. They wanted change now. And they weren't prepared to wait.

The mood on the streets of Halifax during this period mirrored the emerging struggle for black civil rights in the

U.S., and Rocky tapped into that. He invited representatives from the Black Panthers to Nova Scotia. And when the Panthers arrived, everything changed. They said they were prepared to do what they'd been doing in the U.S. — to force systemic change by any means necessary.

The Panthers brought the real possibility of organized, black-led violence to Halifax. Their tactics went beyond marching, singing, praying and demonstrating for change. For the first time, there was a real possibility that black people were going to physically push back. It was not "business as usual."

The possibility of black violence scared the hell out of the city of Halifax and the Halifax Police Department. But it also scared a lot of black people in the community. Not every black person was on board for radical change, especially if it included violence. Many of the older black community members did not support this approach. The threat of violence had never been used before, and the outcome of such tactics was totally unknown.

In 1968, intercommunity discussions culminated in a "blacks only" meeting at the North End Public Library. For our community to talk among ourselves, to the exclusion of white people, was an extremely radical action at that time. Actually, it was unheard of.

The meeting was convened to discuss whether the community should go the route of the Black Panther Party or continue with what we'd been doing — which was to say, working within the system.

For the Panthers, the people who needed the most help were going to get the most help, and the mistreatment of black people, especially by the police, was going to stop. If that took a show of force, that's what they were prepared to offer. The Panthers' process meant there would be individual sacrifices to bear, such as loss of employment, incarceration or physical injury. It might also mean being stigmatized and isolated.

On the other hand, there was the status quo option — that of working within the system. It meant more focus groups and meetings with the city and with the police. In the past, this approach had only ever yielded a few crumbs from white society's table. We made demands, but at the first signs of white resistance, we accommodated and withdrew, only to repeat the process again at a later date.

In 1968, at the library meeting, we were asking ourselves whether we were collectively comfortable with the crumbs from white society's table, or whether we were ready for a new setting. We asked ourselves whether we were still comfortable living on the plantation, or whether we were ready to overthrow the master. Ultimately, the community decided that they weren't going to go the way of the Panthers. But the very fact that this meeting in the library took place, coupled with the Panthers being in town, had a huge impact on the white establishment in Halifax, especially in relation to how our community was being policed.

On an early summer day in 1968, I was hanging out at Creighton and Gerrish Street, one of my favourite corners, with a good friend, Ricky Smith. As we often did, we were "playing the dozens." The term refers to the days of slavery, when substandard slaves would be sold by the dozen, which was considered the deepest of insults. Playing the dozens, in the modern day, meant throwing insults at each other and learning to take it without becoming physical or taking the game too seriously. It could be a joke about what you were wearing or a joke about one of your more noticeable bodily features. It could be a "yo mamma" joke. It could be about losing your girlfriend to someone else. It could be any insult you could think of. This organized abuse, dished out among ourselves, allowed — and still allows — black people to build up a tolerance to the real abuse that we are inevitably forced to take from white society.

As Ricky and I stood there, Donny Young, who worked on the railroad with my father, pulled up in his Lincoln car. In the back seat was Parker Borden, who worked in the community and was around quite a bit. Buddy Daye, an ex-boxer and community leader whom I regularly saw at the Creighton Street gym, was sitting across from Parker in the back seat. These were three black men who lived in the community, who wanted to improve the lot of black people.

Donny pulled up right in front of Ricky and me and said, "C'mon, get in boys. We're going somewhere."

I was a bit nervous; before I get in somebody's car, I've always liked to know where I'm going. But I wasn't scared. These guys were community people. I asked them what was going on, and I remember Donny saying, "Why don't you just get in and keep quiet?"

Ricky and I looked at each other, shrugged our shoulders, then got into the front seat. We were driven down to the police station, which at the time was on Brunswick Street. I'd kept my nose clean, so it was the first time I'd ever been there.

We were led down a squeaky clean hallway into what seemed like a prearranged meeting with Verdon Mitchell, then the chief of police. He was meticulous in his dress and manner. He was a man who paid attention to details. Well spoken. Very professional. Ex–Royal Canadian Mounted Police. I had no absolutely idea what was going on.

Verdon, Donny, Parker and Buddy began a dialogue about the black community, specifically about what could be done about policing the black community and what wouldn't work. Buddy talked about his experiences in the merchant marines. It was a general back-and-forth banter that lasted about ninety minutes. Ricky and I just sat there and listened to the entire conversation. We didn't say a word. Finally, at some natural break in the conversation, Buddy looked hard at Ricky and me. Without taking his eyes off of us, Buddy said to Chief Mitchell, "Perhaps you can give these two young men summer jobs."

Summer jobs?

Excuse me?

My gut feeling is that Ricky and I were a spontaneous afterthought to this meeting. I think that Donny, Parker and Buddy were headed along to their meeting with the chief, and just happened to see us on the corner. I figure they saw us and just then and there decided to bring us along with them. It helped that Ricky and I were both uninvolved in the riots and conflict going on around us at the time. Looking back, if you were to see us, standing there, given the proper political turmoil unfolding around us, you might also think to yourself, "Yeah, those two could be future cops."

That being said, I don't think that Donny, Parker and Buddy were looking for us. I also don't think that Chief Mitchell expected this request from Buddy.

Their decision to bring me along to that meeting was to have a great impact on my life. At nineteen, still in high school, I was to be thrust into the eye of the storm that was pitting the city police against the black community. What I didn't know then — but what I do know now — was that I was a bargaining chip. On the one side, there was Donny,

Parker and Buddy offering up the possibility of Ricky and me as young police officers to Chief Mitchell. On the other side was the fear of the dark — the unknown of the Black Panther Party. We were just two little pieces of a puzzle, but the message to the white power structure was clear — put these boys in uniform, or the alternative might be more than you can handle.

CHAPTER 2
BOXING LIFE

As a young boy, my father introduced me to the art of boxing. He'd sit on the kitchen chair, and he'd give me these oversized boxing gloves to put on. I'd try to hit him and he'd duck and weave, give me a soft punch and push me off. I loved these exchanges; day after day I'd keep coming back for more. This was an era when physical contact between black males often didn't extend much beyond a handshake, and these punching sessions in the kitchen bridged the gap between father and son. They meant the world to me.

My father was a porter on the railroad, and he later became a conductor. In the black community at that time, with the limited opportunities that were available, being a porter was considered a respected, almost prestigious job. Many of my father's black friends — and some white ones — worked the rails with him. His job involved making beds, serving meals and generally tending to the needs of the mostly white clientele on their overnight train trips.

He travelled three days a week on the overnighter from Halifax to Montreal, then back home. When I was a kid, from time to time he took my mom and I with him. When we travelled, we were given our own roomette, and we were waited on by the staff and served with the heavy silver utensils and the thick fine china. I remember the fragrances coming from the kitchen car. I'd peer in and watch the cooks preparing the meals about to be served. I remember the gentle rocking of the train as it meandered through the thick, seemingly endless forests of the northern New Brunswick landscape; I count these trips as some of my happiest memories.

As a teenager, I'd go down to the old train station in the South End. Prior to the train's departure, I'd help my dad make up the upper and lower berths. I felt a sense of pride helping him at his job, and I aspired to one day get a job as a porter as well. I suspect, however, that my dad wanted me far away from the realities of the railroad. The abuses that he had to endure during his lifetime dulled the romance of the big engines and the cross-country trips.

Dad was a hard man. He was a stern taskmaster who demanded excellence of me to the point of over control. Around the house, he would sometimes assert himself to the point of aggressiveness. I knew it was coming from a place of love, but sometimes after work he just couldn't relax. Between the abuse from white patrons on the railroad, the non-stop gossip from our nosier neighbours and the pain of his family-of-origin issues, mentally he was stretched thin.

My father couldn't express his emotions, which I think is a relatively common condition among black men. Racist society dismissed his pain as irrelevant and unimportant and therefore without social remedy or recourse. With

Calvin, thirteen years old, at summer camp in 1966.

expressions of pain unavailable to him, my dad turned towards one of the few emotional options open to him — anger. This anger, with its root causes unacknowledged, slowly turned to rage. This rage, without an outlet, was subsequently internalized and became depression. The depression, overwhelming at times, sought to be numbed. In his case, my father turned to alcohol. The fear, disillusionment, hopelessness and helplessness that he must have often felt was not shared. He kept that to himself.

When you can't process your emotions, how can you tell your own child how they'll *feel* the first time a white person calls them a nigger? Because it will happen. And so instead of learning these lessons, we boxed in the kitchen. Punching each other because we didn't know how to hold each other and cry. During those intimate moments, we connected.

Today in our communities, the emotional detachment continues. Many black men remain guarded in their sharing of emotions. They abuse drugs and alcohol to kill the pain. We live our lives like animals, in our exterior environments, not venturing inside of our ourselves. Letting one's guard down, for an instant, could have dire consequences. So we become hypervigilant, constantly scanning our environment for opportunities and threats. Just learning to take a punch, you develop a resilience to external stressors, until the pain is normalized and living under constant stress becomes standard.

There are very few white psychologists or support groups that can provide black people with professional help to deal with our emotions, from a black perspective. They will never understand the daily attacks on our dignity that we suffer as a result of racist behaviour. They can only understand this experience from an intellectual standpoint, not an emotional standpoint. And so they cannot reach us.

I grew up in a neighbourhood where there were gang fights. We didn't use knives or guns back then. We used our fists. I was a meek and shy young man, and I was terrified of being beaten up. My lack of confidence betrayed me. I was a target for bullies and I was regularly chased — hunted, really — on my way to and from school.

At school I was picked on horribly. The black kids and the white kids in my own neighbourhood bullied me regularly. I couldn't focus on school and failed grades six and eight. I was adrift mentally, a daydreamer, imagining a more peaceful existence for myself. If my father was home from the rails when I came home bruised and crying, he'd scold me for not standing up for myself. He berated me for my fear of physical confrontation. He would be so disappointed with me for not having the capacity to commit physical

The community YMCA basketball team at South Park Street in Halifax in 1965.

violence and for my failure to fight back. He would tell me, "Learn to take a little bit of verbal abuse, but if you've got to fight, then get in that first punch. And make it a hard one."

There was a crew of black youth in my neighbourhood. We'd meet and roam the streets, finding things to do with our spare time. On Saturday afternoons, we'd head over to the boxing gym on Creighton Street. It was a community fixture. Looking back on it, the place was really just a rickety shack with a ring and a few punching bags inside. For showering, there was a stool and a bucket of water in the corner. For heat in the winter, there was a potbellied wood stove. Everyone smoked cigarettes. But all the up-and-coming boxers in Halifax and beyond would go there to train.

And that place made champions! That crummy gym produced a lot of first-rate fighters. Eventually, that included me.

Keith and Percy Paris were the ex-boxer brothers who owned and ran the gym. My friends and I would sit around watching men spar in their headgear, with the sweat pouring off of them. The boxers in the ring took it very seriously, but amidst the slap of their punches connecting, we'd hear them bantering back and forth. It was their second home, where they could relax and test their skills against each other. I began to see that in the art of boxing, there was equality. In the ring, skin colour and race meant absolutely nothing.

When things settled down and the crowds thinned out and the ring was momentarily empty, we kids would put on the too-big boxing gloves and try to knock each other silly. We had few, if any, boxing skills. Keith Paris would laugh at us and say, "You guys are just trying to kill each other!"

My group of friends drifted on, filling their days with basketball, track, football or whatever other activities they could find. But I stayed behind and stuck with boxing. I headed to the gym every spare moment I had, and I found myself learning the basic techniques. There was always somebody around the gym who'd show me something, how to hit the bag, how to skip, how to do routines. I started with shadow-boxing, then sparring drills, then the heavy bag work. I was also taught how to use the speed bag. As a thirteen- and fourteen-year-old kid, I spent most of my free time at the gym, and the boxers became my friends. For motivation at home, I put a picture of Cassius Clay punching Doug Jones in the face, from their 1963 fight, on my bedroom wall.

The last punch I ever allowed myself to take was from a neighbourhood kid named Barry. From a distance, a group of neighbourhood kids had spied me walking home and had given chase. This time, for some reason, I didn't run. I let them approach me. They began to berate me verbally and, as usual, there were racial overtones to the abuse. Barry hauled back and punched me. It was a surprise, because I had done nothing to these kids. I was angry and confused and ran home in tears.

Despite beginning to understand *how* to fight, I couldn't bring myself *to* fight. My mom, in her efforts to seek some kind of justice, called the police. The police officer told me to lay an assault charge. So we went through the process. The court date rolled around, Barry pleaded guilty, and the judge fined him twelve dollars and seventy-five cents.

After that, the bullying just got worse. Going to court was no deterrent for the kids on the street. Half the people didn't know I'd even gone to court, and the other half didn't care. The name-calling didn't stop. The harassment didn't stop. I became determined to make it stop on my own.

The next person who tried to pick on me was Carl, another of my regular tormentors. He'd been verbally abusive before, and we'd had a couple of minor confrontations. But this time was different. He started off with his usual insults about my skin colour.

"Your face is dirty! Wipe it off!"

I stopped and looked at him. Enough was enough. I slammed my fist into his face. He pushed me against a parked car. I pushed him back against a house and slammed his head into the side of the building. He stopped fighting, stumbled and leaned on the car, winded. I delivered a left hook to his body, and he doubled over on the ground. I could see he'd had enough. His friends were shocked with what I had done. I was shocked with what I had done too.

I'll always remember that day, not only for fighting back, but also because I drove the first knuckle of my baby finger back into my right hand, breaking it. Word went around the neighbourhood that I'd fought and fought well. My mental toughness was finally catching up with my physical toughness. The bullying stopped immediately.

As I continued to box, I got to meet some of the local champions. There was Cecil Gray and Clyde Gray, who became professional champs. There was Sherry Lawrence, an up-and-coming boxer in Nova Scotia, and David Downey, who still holds the record for the longest time as the Canadian middleweight champion, and Lenny Sparks, who became a Canadian welterweight champion. These people were constantly at the gym, honing their skills, working out. All around me, there were plenty of black male role models in the community, but these men stood out for me because of their work ethic and dedication. They showed me what I'd need to do to become a competent boxer, and the sweat and blood that had to go into it.

As I got a bit older and got to know David Downey better, he would take me around to the other gyms in town. David became a constant in my life. We'd go from the Creighton Street gym to the gym in the Industrial Building at the Halifax Forum Complex. Then we'd go hit the gym at the Stadacona Naval Base on Gottingen Street, the gym in Mulgrave Park in the housing project in the North End and the gym on Barrington Street. We'd be working out two, sometimes three times a day. Each gym had its own personality and composition of people training, watching and just hanging out. I'd spar with Dave and all the other would-be fighters.

Sherry Lawrence would have me over to his house. We'd go out to the backyard and box. We'd be alone in the yard, just me with my enthusiasm and him with his skills. He was a much better boxer than me, and so when I got cocky and thought I might slip a punch in on him, he'd put me back in my place with a flurry of punches I'd never even see coming. And I'd go home with a headache and a glass of milk.

In sparring, taking punches is part of the learning process. Of course, we all try to take the fewest punches possible, but inevitably I learned to, as they say, roll with them. In many ways, learning to take a punch saved me from myself. It was never just an engagement of fisticuffs; learning to take a hit and not get knocked off your game plan was a lesson that would support me all my life.

At that time in Nova Scotia, amateur boxing wasn't organized in any coherent fashion. There were no amateur tournaments. Boxers at the gyms were either looking to work out and stay fit or were trying to go professional and make a career out of it. If you wanted to be a fighter, you had to fight professionally. There was no middle ground.

I had talents that were starting to develop. I don't know if I had what it took to go pro, but my father would have stood in my way if I'd even tried. He envisioned something different for me, something other than fighting another man in the ring for my pay. Going pro, however, was seen by many in the black community as a way to make a good living beyond menial labour. It was also a way to realize dreams of fame and glory.

From the perspective of poverty, and black poverty in particular, striving for economic advancement through sport — and also entertainment — is a global phenomenon. The great black boxing champions that have come out of Nova Scotia fit this pattern. White society, for its part, generally won't stand in the way of these efforts. Black actors and athletes are nonthreatening to white society because white people still own the teams, the venues and the production companies. A black athlete might enrich him or herself through perseverance and skill, and a black entertainer might share their respective skills on the stage, but the racial stratification of labour and employment remains unchallenged.

But aspire to be the mayor? Or the chief of police? Or the top scientist at a university? That's different. Strive for real influence and power, and you will be met with resistance from a powerful segment of white society.

I didn't go pro. But I kept up my training, and I sparred with everyone and anyone that I could. The gym was a safe zone for me, free from the escalating racial conflict everywhere else. For me, it was a necessary respite. Outside of the gym, we were constantly dealing with issues of racial conflict. The police patrolled the community and stalked the streets. Some were doing their jobs while others were hunting blacks to satisfy their racial biases and beef up their quotas.

So sure, maybe the same anger that haunted my own father haunts me too. Maybe the same inability to express emotion has been passed down through the generations. Maybe my knees are ruined from too many shadow-boxing sessions at sunrise, and maybe we all get worn down by the system in the end. My punching on a bag until my knuckles bleed changes none of this. But I've never had a drink in my life, and I'll go out fighting all the same.

An uninitiated observer might see a boxing match as a contest between two hyperaggressive individuals, pummelling on each other until one falls over unconscious. But that's not it at all. Aggression gets you hurt. Aggression is throwing caution to the wind. With aggression, you set no boundaries on your actions and you lose control. If you lose control, you lose the fight. Assertiveness, on the other hand, is you knowing when and where to set a boundary and knowing how to enforce that boundary. Assertiveness keeps you safe. Assertiveness makes you a thinking fighter, inside the ring and out.

To be clear, I don't believe that we are put on the earth to hit each other. There's a bigger goal for people in sports, whether it's boxing or running up and down the field with a football or kicking a soccer ball. The self-discipline, the training and the development of self-confidence lead to something else. They're skill sets that will serve you well in the great arena of life.

All the same, to me it's a shame that the interest in boxing is waning for young black men. Our communities have been weakened under the dual impacts of drugs and gentrification. The community gyms used to be places where life lessons could be passed from one generation to the next. Sadly, I see them boarding their windows and closing their doors. Suburban mega-gyms, perfect and clean, might offer boxing lessons as some small part of their membership packages. But these high-priced venues, on the outskirts of town, are inaccessible, geographically and financially, for most black youth.

I started off as a kid watching men from the community box each other, then go out for a beer afterwards, no hard feelings. They didn't carry grudges that ended in gunplay and funerals, and I could see the work and discipline that went into their training. It was an honest way to settle differences, based on skill and determination, that now too often end in gunfire.

I saw boxers like Dave Downey, on his way to becoming a champion, take a shower by standing on a piece of plastic and having a bucket of cold water poured over him. That's humility. And those are the shoulders on which I stood. I would have liked the chance to pass that on to the next generation.

Most of the people I knew who were involved in boxing, old-timers now, are still involved. They've gone back to the community, or they're not far from it. There is a core of people who, through boxing, have generated community awareness and community pride in Nova Scotia. And that's what happens when you accomplish something from humble beginnings. But without the youth to pass this along to, we are just a bunch of old men boring you with our fading memories.

When you look at martial arts gyms around the world, they're still out in the backyards. They've kept their community gyms vibrant as places of learning. These enclaves not only build skills, they build character. Many of the practitioners don't have the money, time or transportation to go beyond their immediate environment to practice their skills, so they build their gyms where they are. They invest what they have in the places where they are.

CHAPTER 3
WALKING BLACK, WHITE AND BLUE LINES

In the fifties and sixties, I saw black men, like my father and his friends, full of self-confidence. They went out in the evenings with their wives. They went about their business to the banks and stores. My father bought his clothes from stylish men's shops in Montreal on his layovers.

I saw these men get up and go to work and do it over and over and over again, every day, for their whole lives. They were polite when they could be and assertive when they had to be. But despite their work ethic and their professionalism, the opportunities for black people were very limited in Nova Scotia. In my youth, I lived next to a fire station, but I never saw a black fireman. I rode the bus, but I never saw a black bus driver. I got sick, but I never saw a black doctor. We were all conditioned to think that these were white men's jobs and to not even bother filling out an application form. And until that meeting with Chief Mitchell, it had never occurred to me that I could be a cop either. The best I could imagine was making up a white man's bunk on his train trip to Montreal, or perhaps punching for my life in the ring.

Layton Johnson, from East Preston, was the first black cop in Nova Scotia. Layton was hired in 1967, the very year the Black Panthers came to Halifax. Fancy that.

This was the first time that the police department had ever opened its doors to hiring a black person. Before then, it was

Calvin's application mugshot for Halifax City Police was taken at Halifax City Police Station on Brunswick Street in 1969.

a whites-only institution. In quick succession, with the city in damage-control mode, John Morrison and Ricky Smith were hired in 1968, then Max Hartley and myself in 1969 and Winston Jackson shortly after that. We were the unlikely cubs of the Black Panther Party's time in Nova Scotia.

I remember the first time I saw Layton directing traffic. He was at the intersection of Cornwallis and Gottingen Streets. It was absolutely incredulous to see a black man in a police officer's uniform. He didn't need to direct traffic; traffic just stopped to look at him. Instead of going about our business, we all just dropped everything we were doing to stare. He may as well have been an alien come down from another planet. There were people on every corner. It was unheard of for Halifax.

What were people thinking?

"Well, this is great." Or perhaps, "Now, this is progress!"

Or, "Would you look at this nigger in a position of authority."

Because of the long history of police intimidation in Nova Scotia, and a general view that the police were an extension of the government, around the community there was a whole lot of negative talk going on after Layton became a cop. The episodes of racial unrest and violent clashes with certain white police officers were fresh — and ongoing — in the community's mind. Having one of our own walk the streets as a police officer wasn't seen as the beginning of the radical change that some in the community wanted. In fact, there was chatter that blacks in cop uniforms weren't even a step in the right direction at all. And for those willing to give it a chance, one black man in uniform did not remove the general mood of suspicion towards the Halifax police.

When I look back and ask myself whether the police department would have hired black officers when they did if there hadn't been political unrest in the community, my answer is hell no. Not a chance. Over the years, different people on the force have told me that there had been previous qualified black applicants who'd put in for police jobs. Before the Panthers showed up, the standard procedure for dealing with a black applicant was to thank him, then throw his application in the wastebasket and laugh at him once he walked out the door.

There was no softening of the rotten core of white supremacy. Rather, the hiring of black officers was a panicked reaction of the white power structure to the suddenly real threat of black radicalism in Halifax. We black officers were hired because the government was scared shitless and was looking to put black faces in the right places. I call this the "colour connection." We were tokens. And tokens by definition replace the real thing. Tokenism only benefits the individual token, not the masses. Back then, though, I was totally unaware that the opportunity I had just been handed was so politically loaded. The way I saw it, no other job was going to give me, a black teenager, a uniform, a salary and the perception of a meaningful career. Given my lack of career options, I thought I'd try being a cop.

While this reactionary hiring spree was taking place, grass-roots voices within the community were developing and promoting options for alternative justice models. Rocky Jones and others pitched a program to the police department where black people who had committed certain crimes, instead of being charged and sent to jail, would be turned over to the black community for a measure of justice. Rocky and his people would provide mentorship and get offenders "straightened out," rather than having the system turn them into career criminals. They didn't call it restorative justice back then, but the processes they were advocating for followed that general model. This was also the side of the community that saw no use in the hiring of black police officers. Or, for that matter, any police officers at all. Black officers or no, for them policing was merely the most physical extension of the racist system.

After our meeting with Vernon, Buddy and Parker, Chief Mitchell dropped Ricky and me off at our homes. It was the first ride I'd ever had in a police car. Within a few days we were contacted and, true to his word, Mitchell gave us our promised summer jobs.

I started in the detective office, and Ricky went to the traffic office. I figured I had the better job because Ricky was working handing out traffic tickets, and I was immersed in the world of crime-solving. I was in a general state of confusion as to what was actually going on around me. It was as though somebody in the casting department had made a mistake and had let a black youth onto the set of a for-television police station. Except this was real. Here I was, just nineteen, walking into a room full of big, tough-looking white detectives in suits, while a steady flow of alleged offenders and victims came in and out of the office, giving statements or getting questioned.

By virtue of being black, sometimes Ricky and I were added into police line-ups for victims to identify their perpetrators. On several occasions, one of us was picked out of the line-up as the criminal. Whenever this happened, the whole office would have a good laugh at our expense.

Being inquisitive, I used to look up the names of people I knew who had been charged and read the circumstances of their arrests and convictions. Nobody was really keeping tabs on me, so I'd find an unused corner of the station and flip through folders and take a look at their mugshots. As a nosy youth, it was fascinating to read how kids in the community had gotten arrested and what they'd done. It also gave me a look into the inner workings of the detective office.

Sometimes the political turmoil on the streets made its way into the police station. During that first summer stint, two plainclothes RCMP officers showed up at the station and asked me to be an informant for their bureau. In full view and earshot of the rest of the detective staff, they asked me to give them a call if I should hear of any significant political planning in the works within the black community. I guess they figured that, simply by being black, I would be on the inside of any planning processes. Halifax wasn't RCMP jurisdiction, but the situation with the Black Panther Party would, in today's terminology, probably be classified as an act of national terrorism. Documents that later surfaced through the Access to Information process have shown that the RCMP were very active on the Black Panther Party case file.

As an informant, personally I would have been useless. Usually, the more criminally oriented a person is, the better informant they make. I wasn't a goodie-goodie, but I was home and in bed by ten o'clock and had absolutely nothing to inform about. I wasn't into any kind of crime or any kind of political activity of any substance.

To put the situation of 1968 into perspective, the Halifax police had just formed a riot squad specifically to deal with the imagined future of violent black unrest. The force had gone out and purchased extra large patrol wagons with bench rows for mobile lockups in preparation for the mass street riots they figured were inevitable. The cops were readying themselves for urban warfare; blacks were the enemy. While today riot squads and hypermilitarized policing units are the norm, especially when dealing with crowd control, at the time we hadn't seen anything like it before.

On one occasion, I was brought in to hold the spotlights for some kind of propaganda video the police department was shooting of the riot squad being formed. They were running through preparedness exercises, on camera, I guess to appear tough and ready to deal with the "black menace." Leo Storm, then one of the sergeants, joked to me that the force didn't want anyone in the black community to know that they were forming a riot squad. Yet there I was, holding the spotlight for their videos.

At that age, I didn't realize the unspoken nuances of what would be expected of me in the future, or of the conflicts that I would have to navigate. Honestly, I just loved the thrill of the job. And while it was clearly a make-work project, without any real duties or serious responsibilities, the intensity and excitement in the detective's office was something I knew I had to have more of.

The summer of '68 ended — without the anticipated race riots — and I went back to high school. But I knew I wanted to be a cop.

My having worked at the police station over the summer made a number of people suspicious of me. They figured that since I had had that summer job, I must by default be a high school informant, constantly in communication with the police, telling the cops what was going on in the community. A number of kids my age started calling me an Uncle Tom and a "white man's nigger." They said I couldn't be trusted. That I was an outsider now. That I was finished in the community. At nineteen, this wasn't the easiest thing to hear. However, there were other black people in the community who were supportive of me and expected me to practice good policing in the community once I became a police officer. That being said, I still wonder what black people in the community meant when they said, "We want black cops."

Did they want black cops who would treat them with dignity and respect because they were being assaulted and abused on the streets by certain white police officers?

Did they think that a few black cops — us tokens — would be able to replace a deeply racist system with justice and equality?

Did they want black cops to let them do what they wanted because "we're all black"?

Did they want someone who would give them a pass, with a wink and a nod, when they did something wrong?

Ricky Smith, being twenty-one, managed to enroll with the Halifax police right after our summer gig, in the fall of 1968. I was still in high school and had to finish my final year. In September of '69, I enrolled in the Halifax City Police's three-month recruitment class. I was the senior man in the class because I had done the summer placement the year before. We were told the good, the bad and the ugly of how we, as new police officers, were expected to conduct ourselves in public. We were trained with wooden batons, handcuffs and revolvers, and that was basically it. Our homework was to learn the criminal code, the provincial statutes and local and municipal laws.

We also had self-defence classes and firearms training. My physical abilities were better than many of the other recruits because by this point I'd been boxing since I was thirteen. Within a few years, I became the boxing instructor for the police self-defence course.

We were told that we would be scrutinized, seven days a week, twenty-four hours a day, on the job and off the job. As a black youth in this relatively unique position, navigating my own community as a new police officer was like learning to swim by being tossed into the Atlantic. There was no warm-up, no preamble and there was no walking from the shallow end to the deep end. There were also no seasoned black police officers from whom I could seek guidance and learn these nuances. In 1969, our elder black officer, Layton Johnson, had only been a cop for two years. And by the time I became a full-time cop, he had moved on from the Halifax police. I was given a uniform, thrown into this turmoil of racial strife on the streets and expected to implicitly understand what the hell to do. It was like walking a tightrope.

As recruits, for two weeks in mid-training we walked the beat with seasoned police officers before we went back to our classroom education. The beat was where we separated theory from reality. We learned the different styles each police officer had in dealing with the public, in real time. Of course, all of our mentors were white cops. Some were very abrasive and verbally abusive in their dealings with the black community. Others were more persuasive in their approach, getting voluntary compliance through verbal intervention. Some officers were respectful, and some were downright ignorant and exacerbated situations with their body language and verbal cues.

In one particular instance, a police officer I was training with stopped a vehicle on Gottingen Street. The black man behind the wheel had done nothing wrong, but the officer demanded his licence in a condescending, authoritarian way. I was standing next to him as this cop took the licence, glanced it over and said, "That's not your licence!" as he tossed it back at him.

Remember, I was just treading water here, adrift in the ocean. As a twenty-year-old recruit, I couldn't tell the officer to check his attitude and not throw the man's driver's licence back at him. As a new recruit, I wasn't going to have the backing of management or any of my white fellow officers if I said anything, so I just had to take it all in. Yet here I was, in the same uniform as my abusive colleague, representing the same system. And my silence was my complicity. This guy, just driving his car, had just been treated like shit by not one, but two police officers, for no reason other than being black. His abuse had no recourse. And he just had to bury his anger.

As my training went on, I saw instances such as this take place repeatedly. And when I was off shift, sitting around the kitchen table or hanging out in the neighbourhood, the black community would tell me stories about individual cops being abusive. I knew those cops, and I knew their views. The community wasn't wrong, and I came to understand why some in the black community simply hated the police — as an institution.

Upon graduation, we new recruits "hit the beat" and spent about three months getting to know the secrets of Halifax's neighbourhoods, step by step. Literally. The beats were named after street intersections where there would be a police call box. Back in the day, these call boxes were the beat cop's lifeline to the central station.

You opened the call box with a skeleton key that every officer was given. Inside, there was a telephone, and you

Calvin's graduating class photo for Halifax City Police was taken at Halifax Police Station on Brunswick Street in 1969.

would check in every hour with the "station house," where there was a dispatcher at a switchboard in the police station who would patch you in and accept your calls. You would then stand by at the call box for ten minutes, in case the station house needed to contact you and send you out on a specific call. Most of the time, the calls you received on the beat were related to break and enters or traffic issues.

Sergeants were the officers in charge. There were three sergeants on each platoon, and there were three platoons that worked the different shifts. A platoon was comprised of approximately twenty-five or thirty people. My sergeants were Mitchell, Cuthbert and White. They would come around and check on me and the rest of the platoon while

Calvin's 1969 graduation photo.

we walked the beat. We would have regular interactions with them, so I came to know the specifics of what each of them was like, personally, and I grew to know what the on-the-job expectations were. They kept an eye on us and made sure we didn't get out of line. Not infrequently, young new cops had to be mentored, verbally disciplined or simply reined in. Each beat had its own personality, and each of the three shifts had its own characteristics. Halifax was (and still is) a bustling port city with shipyards, residential areas, vibrant club scenes, wealthy South End neighbourhoods and, during the swinging sixties, hippie hangouts. By virtue of demographics and geography, you couldn't just patrol each beat in the same manner.

If management wanted to catch you in dereliction of your duties, they'd have one of the sergeants sit behind a door in a commercial area, in the dark, waiting for you to come along and rattle the doorknobs to make sure that the local businesses were locked up for the night. This was implicitly understood as one of your job duties. If you didn't turn that doorknob to make sure that it was locked — if one of the sergeants was hiding in there — you were charged with neglect of duty. In the wintertime, the sergeants would come along and follow at some distance and time delay. If they didn't see your footprints in the fresh snow, they determined that you hadn't walked your beat, which could again result in disciplinary action. If you called in sick, the sergeant would drive to your house to see if you were actually sick. And if you didn't check in at the call box every hour, or if you left the beat for any reason, you could expect repercussions from the sergeant.

Through this education, I came to learn that the foundation of community policing is walking the beat. The streets are where everything happens, and where communication and building trusting relationships with the community are paramount. I learned that the cop walking the beat should be nosy, should be inquisitive, should talk to people, should go in and out of stores and should engage people in conversation. Issues in the community get noticed by a good beat cop, working all three shifts — the midnight to eight, the eight to four and the four to midnight. After six months of that kind of immersion in a community, the observant beat cop will know everything there is to know about a particular area.

Some people say that walking the beat is passé. I hear them say that it's not cost-effective, and that the days of beat cops are gone. They tell me it's not efficient in relation to the many duties that cops today are expected to perform. They tell me policing has changed. And I must disagree.

Advancements in technology may be good, but not simply by virtue of introducing flashy new bells and whistles that cut costs and claim to render certain duties redundant. To me, any technology that reduces a cop's face-to-face time with the public is counterproductive. When you're staring at a screen, allowing a predictive model, rather than the voice of the community itself, to determine where you should patrol, you're limiting your exposure to the public and vice versa. When you're walking the beat, you're talking to the people. You're talking to the criminals. To the children. To the people who have mental issues. To the shop owners. You hear the community's issues and concerns, and, if you're actually listening, you adjust your policing habits accordingly.

Walking the beat gives you a deep and intimate knowledge of a community. And it can't be replaced by more invasive, publicly unpopular techniques like CCTV or random street checks. These technologies and tactics are adversarial. In my time walking the beat, I caught people breaking into buildings. I caught people damaging property. I caught people breaking into vehicles. And I wasn't behind a desk or in a police car. I wasn't even on a bicycle. I was walking the streets.

After I became a sworn officer, it became my turn to walk with the new recruits, training them on the beat. I remember walking with a recruit on Gottingen Street on the four-to-midnight shift. There were a lot of people milling about. I was casually talking to the people on the street, just making small talk. I wasn't being cordial and pleasant because I was a black cop in a black neighbourhood. I was chatting — respectfully and empathetically — because communication is the foundation of any relationship. I prided myself on my approach. It was an approach grounded in understanding that escalated enforcement is a final, not first, resort.

The recruit working with me couldn't believe what I was doing. He told me that the last officer with whom he had trained had treated Gottingen Street like it was some kind of war zone. He spoke to no one. He kept his head down, his body tensed and ready for the confrontation he was anticipating.

In my day, these officers were invariably white, but this isn't a white or black thing. I've worked with a lot of quality white police officers — Curt Taylor, Dave Pike and Calvin Cluette, to name a few. These guys were not from the black community and had never worked in a black community. But they did it as well as any police officer, black or white. They had a respect and a feel for the people. The black community knew which cops were there for the benefit of the community, and which officers were there to "go hunting." On the flip side, I've seen some black cops be harder than a white cop on their own people, just so that they could hear their white supervisors say, "Hey, you're okay. You're one of us."

At the Halifax police station, the general term that got bandied about for the black community was "Charlie Zone," in reference to the ongoing Vietnam conflict. The black community was enemy turf, and our men, women and children were the insurgents. Sheltered against us in the station, every night the police prepared themselves, mentally and physically, to go to war with us rather than walk among us.

So while we are charged with upholding the law, do all communities get policed the same, under the law?

Are laws made or applied equally?

No. Definitely not.

There is a lot of pressure from politicians to have certain areas policed in a certain way. There is a lot of media scrutiny that gets unequally applied to certain areas. In Nova Scotia, these days, when you speak of Mulgrave Park, Uniacke Square, East Preston or North Preston, you're talking about whole communities. Black communities with nuances, subtleties and a range of people and issues as wide and varied as anywhere else. But there's also a well-understood stereotype attached to these areas.

When something criminal happens in those communities, the communities themselves get stigmatized in the media. Rather than a reporter saying "a crime took place on Gottingen Street," you'll hear "a mugging happened in Mulgrave Park," and the entire community becomes criminalized. In this way, the entire community, rather than a specific place and moment in time, gets labelled as a criminal, negative place. A dangerous place. Not a place to raise a family or do business.

Nobody wants to be stigmatized, or to feel the shame of living within a stigmatized community. People living around the periphery of that community don't want to be painted with the same brush, and so they seek to separate themselves, to create a false us-versus-them binary. They work and lobby the city to get the names of the streets changed, to clearly set those boundaries between us and them. For example, the north end of Gottingen Street was renamed Novalea Drive, as if Gottingen Street — and all that was supposedly attached to it — had some kind of arbitrary ending. It's the same street. Creighton Street was changed to Northwood Terrace. Again, the same street.

Now, when something criminal happens on Creighton Street or Gottingen Street, citizens look at their TVs or read the newspaper and say, "Wow. Look at that black neighbourhood. Crime is out of control. I'm glad I don't live there. Better give the police the right to go in there and do whatever they need to do. Get tough on crime." The black community becomes a war zone, the over-policing of "problem" neighbourhoods is legitimized and this vicious spiral is perpetuated by the media.

From my perspective, walking the streets of my community in the late sixties and early seventies, conflict between the police and the black community was smouldering and could have burst into flames at any time. By virtue of the political

situation, my job extended beyond the realm of simple policing and crime-fighting and prevention. I became a virtual
tightrope walker — a double ambassador of the policing
community within the black community, and vice versa.

There were a number of popular nightclubs on Gottingen
Street. There was the Prizefighter's Club, the Gerrish Street
Hall and a variety of other clubs that comprised the entertainment district of the black community. At night, music
flowed out from open doors, and the sidewalks were packed
with people in various states of drunkenness, milling about.
People were everywhere, partying all night and hanging out.
Combined with the general political mood, the whole area
was always a potential powder keg.

The first night I walked the beat there, I was peppered
with insults from black folks.

"Uncle Tom!"

"Sellout!"

That same first night, on the same shift, I had white
people laughing at me and calling me a nigger. Here I was,
twenty years old and taking bullshit from both sides on a
Friday night, just for showing up in uniform to police my
community. My first thought was that I didn't want to come
back there, ever. I was hearing it from all sides, and I didn't
have the time, energy or ability to respond to every insult
or challenge. With all the wisdom of a twenty-year-old, I
said, "Fuck it, that's the way that people are," and I dug in
my heels.

I know of black officers from the community who were
hired later on who couldn't continue to live on Creighton
Street because of the harassment they got from some of their
black neighbours. I can only encourage the black community, as a group, to stop and think about it. If you want that

representation, you have to support it. You can't complain about not seeing black police officers in the community if you chase away black cops who are actually from the community.

Personally, there was no way I was going to move on because of some random name-calling. I had grown up on Gottingen Street. And I wasn't going anywhere. I'd do my four-to-midnight shift and get called every name under the sun. Then I'd go home, change my clothes and go hang with my friends at the clubs, partying and having a good time with everyone else. On the other hand, some people would see me after a shift and say, "Oh, you're back! Are you spying on us now, or what?" Or, "You arrested my brother last week! Next time I see you off duty, I'm gonna kick your ass."

I was always ready for it. But not too many people acted on their threats.

There used to be a popular hang-out on Gottingen Street called the Derby Tavern, and it was busy at all hours of the day and night. The kitchen would be open late; they would serve an order of two "wing steaks" with fries, and everybody would hang out there. After a midnight shift, I'd go over, grab a table and order my steaks. People would spot me and come by and treat my booth like it was the complaints desk at the police station. They'd be asking me, "How come this happened?" "How come that person got arrested?" "What about this?" "What about that?"

It didn't matter that I was sitting there with a hot meal in front of me. I wasn't offended, and I let them speak. I was working for my community through law enforcement, and so answering to my community was part of my job. I later learned that certain people would say, "Calvin didn't just police here and go home to another community after his shift. Calvin stayed here. He lived here."

That meant something to some people.

Nonetheless, I'd get in these heated arguments at the Derby, based on what I had done during my shift.

I'd say, "Look, I'll explain to you what I did. If you have a problem with what I did and the way I did it, then tell me. But if you have a problem with the fact that I enforce the law, then we can't talk, because we have no line of communication. This is what I have to do. Are you telling me that I shouldn't enforce the law? Or are you telling me that I enforced the law improperly? If I did it wrong, then tell me about it. If you're telling me I shouldn't enforce the law, then back off and let me eat my steaks."

There were always these interactions. And the community kept me in check. Still, no matter how much I explained myself, a part of the black community would say, "Shit, this guy's no better than a white cop."

One night, a black man threw a firebomb through a window at the Prizefighter's Club. The police knew who had done it. Upon arriving for my next midnight shift, I was approached by two white detectives who asked me to accompany them into the community and point out the bomb thrower. I knew him and identified him for them. This caused resentment — obviously from the offender, but also from others in the community. But I stand by what I did. The danger of the act itself — throwing a firebomb into a busy club — demanded that I do everything necessary to enforce the law. My allegiance was not to an individual who had just endangered innocent lives, by virtue of the fact that he was a black man. To me, there was no discretion. It wasn't the same as seeing someone carrying an open beer bottle on the street, where a number of factors can dictate a police officer's response. In my view, this guy needed to be identified and arrested.

Just like in any community, there were some hardcore criminals in the black community. I didn't side with them — for being black — over the protection of the larger community, and I would do everything I could to get them off the street. I didn't judge them. That's the job of our Creator. But for my part, I had to stop their behaviour. Black or white, they were not going to hide in and prey on my community.

Part of my policing style was that I always wanted the person I was arresting to know, even if they wouldn't overtly admit it — even if I ended up rolling on the ground with them — that I had tried everything I could to resolve the issue while letting that person save face. Allowing all parties to save face is extremely important in community policing.

I'll give you an example.

The Misty Moon Club on Gottingen Street was always a popular nightspot. They served alcohol — lots of it — and, as it is today, a bar could refuse to serve you if you were too inebriated. And they could call the cops on you if you didn't leave when asked.

Inevitably, on weekends at the Moon, there would be some really drunk guy in the back of the club with his friends. Maybe some fight or confrontation between men had started up mainly because there were women around, and the guys were competing for their attention. I'd get called in and come in the club and suddenly we'd all be face-to-face in the back. There'd be women around, and this drunk guy would have his friends with him, and there I was, a big, black cop tasked with moving him out. He'd always have a number of excuses to try and put on a tough-guy act.

Now, in the back of my mind, I'd know that it would be within my rights as a police officer to just walk over to him and say, "Okay, the management wants you out. They asked you to leave and you wouldn't. Then they called me. So get out."

As a cop, I could have done that and been within the law. But if I had gone about it like that, I wouldn't have been allowing that person to save face. I'd just have been throwing my weight around as a cop. I'd have been breeding hatred in the community, and I'd have been escalating the situation.

Instead, I'd walk over. I'd get down on one knee, keeping in mind my personal safety. And I'd say to this person, "Look, management does have the right to refuse you service. And I don't know what happened here, but they want you to leave. Can you leave for me? I mean you no disrespect."

Now, he'd look around and say, "I'm gonna finish my beer first."

To which I'd respond, "Okay, no problem. I'm just gonna go over there and you can finish your beer."

I'd allow him to save face. I'd allow him to tell me that he was going to finish his beer first. If the guy still didn't want to leave, then I'd have to use a different tactic. But I did give him the opportunity to save face. Maybe the management at the Misty Moon didn't like my style, but the management wasn't going to have to fight with the guy, or hurt him, or get hurt trying, or wind up wasting resources by taking him to court over some preventable infraction. So once it was in my hands, it was going to be done my way. And ultimately, the club didn't want a fight breaking out either. I'd appease everyone and still do my job.

There was another incident, where a well-known woman

from the community had passed out at a table at the El Strado restaurant. I was working the patrol wagon that night, and the police officer walking the beat had decided to arrest her. When I pulled up in the wagon, she was still passed out, so we put her in the wagon and took her to the station. She woke up in one of the holding cells. When she came to, I asked her if there was anything she needed, maybe a phone call, and just she said, "Fuck off."

After my shift, back at the Derby, and out on the streets, people were asking me, "How come you arrested her? Why didn't you leave her alone? She wasn't hurting anybody."

And I replied, "Stop for a second. I didn't arrest her. The beat cop arrested her."

They were saying, "Well, why didn't you take her home?"

They weren't asking me why the management at the El Strado had called the cops in the first place rather than just calling a taxi to take her home. I explained that because I hadn't been the one to arrest her, I had no authority to overrule that decision and let her go. Yes, I had leeway in certain situations. But when I was involved in a process that was already fluid by the time I showed up, there was simply no way I could undo what had already been started.

When you call the police, it's because you want the law involved. But that doesn't mean it's going to be involved on the terms you envisioned. In this regard, having black police officers from the black community makes procedural sense because ideally, they most closely reflect the cultural norms represented in the community, and so can more easily navigate these "grey area" situations and reflect the community's value system. If the first officer on the scene is from the community, and it's just a question of taking someone he or she knows home because they've had too much to drink and they're passed out, then sure, this instance does not need to become a law enforcement issue. In this type of instance, a police officer from the community, with community knowledge, can be a great asset.

Further, as a cop operating in a culture that's not your own, it becomes extremely difficult to comprehend and give meaning to specific cultural behaviours. When you're in a culture that's not your own, you can easily lose your sixth sense. For example, I remember going to a domestic disturbance call in the black community in Uniacke Square. My partner was a white police officer who, in my mind, harboured no racist feelings whatsoever. As is often the case with domestic disputes, there was a lot screaming and hollering. Aside from a lot of noise, nothing was really going on. As a cop, my approach was to wait a bit to give that type of adrenaline-fueled energy time to blow itself out.

In this case, there was a black man in front of us screaming and causing a disturbance. He wasn't doing anything that was physically threatening to anyone or acting out in any other manner. He was just all wound up and yelling. I knew that he could only carry on like that for so long before he tired himself out. So I waited.

Once he'd exhausted himself and stopped for breath, I started calmly talking to him. But when I turned around, my partner had his hand on his holster and was ready to pull his gun. He didn't have his gun out, but he was tense and ready to draw. I understood what had happened. In a black neighbourhood, in a black home, watching a black man yell, this white officer had lost his sixth sense. Suddenly he interpreted everything — including a black man yelling — as being extremely dangerous to him.

When you're hyper-stressed and concerned for your

own safety, you're prone to making mistakes. And officers in foreign cultures, in my opinion, are more apt to become hyper-stressed than officers to whom the culture is common.

This is where the community should have some input on their policing situation. Ideally, police officers should reflect the communities they police. If citizens are demanding more community input into the justice system and the manner in which they are being policed, if I were in a decision-making position, I would allow that input within reasonable parameters. In this way, black cops in black neighbourhoods makes total sense.

The black community, however, has a responsibility here too, insofar as it must take some ownership for what happens on its streets. This doesn't necessarily mean snitching or talking to the police about what happened in a criminal situation. But if you have a relative or a friend selling drugs out of your house or out on the corner, for example — and you know about it — I don't think you have the right to criticize the police when they break down the door and make arrests.

While policing my own community presented a unique dynamic, it wasn't the only one I had to navigate. Being a black cop in a police station filled with white police officers presented its own issues. Many of my co-workers were prepared to judge me solely on the quality of my work, which I did well. Others, however, made it clear that they didn't want to work with a black man under any circumstances.

Back when I served with the Halifax Police Department, the rules were different regarding the use of what you might term "racist language." We didn't have what would now be referred to as a "third party rule." There was no Human Rights Commission. There was no workplace code of conduct regarding racist behaviour. Back in those days, your locker, or your desk, was considered your property. You could put pin-ups of women on your desk, and that was considered your property. Today people have rights and understandably feel offended when they are exposed to racism in the workplace. Now police departments have policies, a corporate mission, a corporate vision and a set of core values for employees. These are some of the checks and balances that are supposed to protect employees from harassment and discrimination.

In my time, if I heard two white cops talking and they used the term "nigger" — and I definitely heard the term all the time — there was nothing I could do about it. They weren't talking to me, so I couldn't seek recourse based on language I had overheard them using among themselves. So I never complained about what I heard being said — and I heard a lot. Talking to my supervisors about the use of racial slurs in the workplace would have been useless because I would have been taking my problem to the problem. Black cops were just coming on the scene, so there was no way to know whether management would be sympathetic to complaints about the use of the word "nigger" by white cops. Some inspectors would be sympathetic, of course. But I also knew that some would not.

A lot of times my fellow officers also did stuff or said things to get a reaction from me. They were "race-baiting" me. And because I had no recourse — and they knew it — I had to deal with it myself. Primarily, I used deflection strategies. This is where my shit-taking ability honed over years of playing the dozens as a kid on the corner came in handy.

I would come back at my tormentors the way they came at me. If they were being insulting, I'd be insulting. If they were going to insult black people, then I'd insult white people. Without a complaints commission or some similar third-party arbiter, I often had to let people say what they wanted to say, to see how far they'd go, to see if they really were racists or just trying words on for size.

In my mind, I had no other choice but to approach it that way, because the minute you challenge somebody or label them a racist, then you have to watch out for them for the rest of your career. My allegations and complaints might have made an impact on their careers. And then I'd have made enemies for life, who would do whatever they could to screw me over. Sure, I also knew that I could have knocked any one of them out cold with my bare hands. But that's aggression, and then I'd have been unemployed. Instead, I had to be assertive, but covertly so. I had to play stupid to make them think I was subservient, so that I could get over on them if the time came when I truly had to. I had to let them think that none of it bothered me.

To be clear, no police officer ever walked up to me and said, in the context of a serious conversation, "Calvin, you're a nigger." And so I had to pick away at the layers — "Is this offensive? Is this not offensive?" At the time, I just let it all slide.

That being said, there were several times when this type of behaviour crossed the line. For example, the Halifax Police Department had their own boat club at the end of South Street, where they'd installed a swimming pool. This was considered a big deal, and for a few weeks there was a poster on the wall at the central police station advertising that the new pool had been built. Someone had written on the poster, "Nigger Bath."

In the police station, we also had what we called the writing room, where we posted mugshots of people who had just been released or had warrants outstanding. And of course, these mugshots were of both black and white individuals.

One day when I went to the writing room, somebody had written "Nigger" and "Coon" and "Calvin Lawrence" over the black mugshots. It was midday by the time I came into the writing room, and so I definitely wasn't the first person to see these slurs written all over the place. To walk in there and know that nobody had said anything about it all morning was a big problem to me. My co-workers' silence on this signalled their complicity.

I wrote a memo to management in which I said, "This is wrong. Not only are police officers seeing this, but people from the public are potentially going to see this. This is not professional."

There was quite a bit of noise made about it as a result of my complaint. Management was going to check handwriting samples to see who had done this, and certain supervisors were saying that whoever it was should be fired.

In response, I said, "Look, I'm not interested in getting anybody fired. What I'm telling you is that what was written on that board was not professional. It's insulting to all black people, not just me. It's insulting to the other black members that work here. And it represents the adversarial relationship this force has to the black community." I had no desire to be a crusader. I just saw something that I didn't like, that was over the line. I didn't overreact. I just brought it to the attention of management.

What I've found, however, throughout the course of my policing career and my life as a black man, is that posting anonymous racial expletives — either as graffiti or as derogatory posters — is one of the favourite tactics of the gutless masses who practice racist behaviour, but who are too afraid of the repercussions to openly express their racist views. It's rare that they'll ever approach you, one to one. Instead, they leave their little messages, or they gossip in their groups where there's safety in numbers.

CHAPTER 4
ILLUSION OF INCLUSION

In boxing, just as in life, the crowds pick their favourites. Hard as it is, in order to be successful, you have to ignore the crowd. The path of your life will ultimately be determined by your mettle and resolve, not by the crowd.

Personally, I am a composite of many things, both inside and outside the ring. When I fought, I was a black boxer. This meant that sometimes the black athletic community would cheer for me, and that the white community would treat me like a villain. But I was also a cop, so sometimes the police community would cheer for me as one of their own, but some of the black community would think I was the enemy. I was dedicated to my boxing training, so my mentors wished success upon me. But I was also a Lawrence, and within the black community there were family resentments, so I had my detractors based solely upon my surname. And of course there were some people I had arrested or had dealt with who carried a grudge against me and wanted to see me get knocked out, whether in the ring or out on the street.

In 1973, when I was twenty-four, Taylor Gordon, a Canadian national boxing coach and dedicated-to-the-hilt trainer, came to Nova Scotia. I remember him arriving at the Industrial Building in the Halifax Forum where I was training. He watched me spar, and he liked what he saw. While I'd never had an actual fight, by this point I had spent years developing my boxing skills. For someone who didn't

Calvin sparring with an Olympic participant in the Industrial Building at the Halifax Forum in 1973.

yet have a fight under their belt, Taylor thought I had some real potential because I had learned the basics.

Taylor was a no-nonsense coach. Either you showed him that you wanted his training methods and that you were ready for his mentorship, or you didn't, and he'd just move on. He didn't coddle you. He approached boxing as though it were a train. If you had a ticket, then it was "All aboard!"

Around that time, Kevin Downey, Dave Downey's nephew, was training alongside me. The Downey family was a boxing dynasty in Nova Scotia. Prior to Taylor's arrival, Kevin and I had been training with his Uncle Dave. We had been sparring partners for years, and we were good friends outside the ring. Our preferred boxing styles, however, were significantly different. I was a slick boxer, a mover, and I didn't exchange punches unless I had to. My strength lay in my jabs and in keeping my opponents off balance, off their game and at a distance. I had a long reach, quick hands and good footwork, and I could control a sparring contest from a distance while using my footwork to tire my opponents out without letting them get at me. Kevin was a more aggressive boxer. He was a slugger, and he had great endurance. He was also a terrific body puncher, and during our sparring rounds he would often get at me, through my defences, and beat on my ribs. On more than one occasion, he had doubled me over with a good body shot.

Taylor went ahead and organized an amateur fight between Kevin and me, and for whatever reason, this didn't sit at all well with the Halifax Police Department. When the department found out that I had a fight scheduled, I was called into the inspector's office and told I wasn't allowed to fight.

I asked whether I was violating any police policies or bringing disrepute to the force.

The inspector responded, "No. No. We just don't want you to do it."

I said, "Well, am I allowed to do it or am I not?"

"Well, technically you're allowed to do it but . . ."

I said, "Well, the fight is already set up now."

"Okay then, just this once. Just this once."

I left perplexed and disappointed. I could feel anger welling inside me. Absent any proper explanation, I immediately suspected racist motives. The inspector claimed that the force didn't mind me training, but that they didn't want me fighting. The only rationale that he offered me to my face was that police policy did not give time off for sporting pursuits.

This confused me because I had never asked for a single hour off of my work schedule to train, spar or anything. I was the "strikes trainer" for the police force, and it was well known around the force that I'd been in boxing training all my youth and adult life. Without a doubt, my boxing skills not only enhanced my own abilities as an officer, but brought a measure of professionalism and physical ability to our staff on the force. Because of my boxing training, I better understood the nature of conflict and was aware of ways to avoid unnecessary physical force. None of that would change if I happened to participate in an amateur boxing match in front of a crowd. I told the inspector this as clearly as I could.

Little did I know that I'd lit a fuse on an even greater conflict.

The Industrial Building at the Forum was packed for the fight. My birth father from Yarmouth and my adopted father were both there. And there we were, Kevin and I, friends, about to step into the ring for a fight. There was a sizeable crowd in the stands, chanting "Beat Calvin!" or "Beat Kevin!"

I tried to take it all in. I figured, "Well, we spar all the time. This shouldn't be a big deal." I figured I could out-box Kevin using my speed, my jabs delivered at a distance and my superior footwork.

In the dressing room, I could hear the crowd yelling. I taped up my hands and shared my confident thoughts on the outcome of the fight with Jerry Burns, another boxer who was there. He said, "Calvin, a fight in the ring is not the same as sparring."

I said "Okay, sure, Jerry." But I didn't take his words to heart. I figured that I would just get out there, beat Kevin and that would be that. In my mind, this was all a done deal.

And then we actually fought. And the only trouble was that nobody told Kevin that he was supposed to lose.

I started off the first round as if we were just sparring, and I thought I was doing pretty well. I moved around, got a few jabs in, and generally stayed out of the way of Kevin's body shots. Then Kevin hit me square in the face with a hard shot. My nose exploded, and I began to bleed profusely. There was blood in my mouthpiece and all over the canvas. My blood was even spattered on the referee's shirt. In a sparring match, a bleeding nose would have stopped the friendly encounter. Here, I didn't have any time to regroup or gather my thoughts. This was a real fight.

At the end of the first round, with me sitting in my corner, I could hear my Halifax father yelling at Taylor because my nose wouldn't stop bleeding.

Then the bell rang again, the stool got whisked out from under me, and it was back into the ring with the crowd cheering for more blood, and Kevin's unrelenting punches to my body. Suddenly, I understood the difference between sparring and the beating I was taking in front of a blood-thirsty crowd. Kevin had come to fight me. I had come to spar with Kevin. And I was being beaten up.

We fought the next two rounds, and Kevin really turned the tables on me. In fact, it felt like he'd hit me with a table. He broke through my footwork and made me fight his fight. Now he was where he loved to be, inside my guard, pounding on my ribs like he was playing a human xylophone. I don't think I hurt Kevin, but I do know he beat me pretty bad. I didn't fall down, but by the time it was over, I was hurting everywhere.

At the fight's end, after three rounds, Kevin whispered in my ear, "Now we can be friends again." This brought me back to reality. It was just a boxing match, and we were two black men from the community.

You cannot have a tie in amateur boxing. In our fight, the judge's scoring took some time because the outcome was close. I gave as good as I could, and I wasn't a pushover. But ultimately, the referee raised Kevin's hand in victory, and I knew it was the right call. He had been by far the more aggressive fighter, and in this case, aggression had won the day. Personally, I was overwhelmed by the entire experience. My ego was devastated at having taken such a bloody loss in front of a big, cheering crowd. It felt like the whole thing was over before I'd even gotten started. I staggered home to tend to my physical and mental wounds.

Taylor Gordon didn't know how I was going to take the loss. Some boxers take their first beating and that's it — they're done after one loss. I can't lie to you; losing like that definitely stung. But, like many twenty-four-year-old males, I was blessed with a lot of pride. So a few days later, after some of my bigger bruises and welts had healed, I was back at the gym ready to go. Upon seeing my humbled frame in the doorway, Taylor just smiled. I hated to lose and said, "Okay. Well, I guess we're going to have to do this dance all over again."

Within a few days, Kevin and I were back sparring again. I had a new respect for the man. A couple of months after that, Kevin dropped his weight down under 187 pounds and he started competing in the light-heavyweight division. I stayed up around 190 pounds, in the heavyweight division. I thought to myself, "Phew. Good. I don't have to fight Kevin anymore." Nevertheless, we continued to spar, and we regularly beat on each other harder than many of our future opponents would.

Officially, there was no response to the fight from management at the Halifax police. But there were threats that I would be taken off the payroll if I got hurt. I pointed out that they hadn't taken officers off of the payroll when they'd gotten hurt playing beer-league baseball on the Halifax Commons, and that in fact I'd covered for them while they were off. Cops got hurt while off-duty all the time — fixing the deck, doing whatever — and they weren't taken off the payroll. And nobody threatened them and pre-emptively told them they weren't allowed to do renovations on their house or fix their own decks.

What it meant was that I was always watching my back, wondering what kind of tactics management might use to stop me from boxing. It became an added pressure on my fighting in the ring. But the hell if it stopped me. I wanted a taste of victory.

I took a couple days of my annual leave when Taylor Gordon scheduled my next match, this time in Toronto.

It was against a man named Brian Nero, a bulky, muscular boxer. He was a fairly slow-moving fighter, but he had a degree of power behind his punches. Over the three rounds, he knocked me off balance a couple of times, but he didn't hurt me in any serious way. Again, though, I just couldn't seem to get my fight started. It was like I was there, in the ring, but not to fight. I couldn't find a reason to get aggressive with him.

There are boxers who will hit anything that moves, but I was never that guy. One of the hardest things I've ever had to do is to mentally prepare myself to fight someone who's done nothing to me. If I didn't have a reason to hit someone, I just didn't seem to have it in me to lay someone out with a punch, even though I could have. I'd been punch-shy against Kevin. And I was punch-shy against Nero. And I lost my second fight by decision.

In my foray into the Canadian amateur boxing circuit, I had now chalked up two consecutive losses. I had all the skills of a fighter, but I wasn't delivering. Walking down the street, the neighbourhood was looking at me funny. In the gym, Taylor was looking at me sideways. And I was looking at myself in the mirror. All of us were wondering, "Does Calvin really want to do this? *Can* Calvin actually do this?"

I had to show up to my next fight to win, or there wasn't any point in continuing down this path.

My third amateur fight was a rematch against Brian Nero. This time we were fighting at home — in Halifax, at the Armoury. There were articles in the local newspapers about the rematch, "0–2 cop boxer looking for rematch . . ." That kind of thing.

At the Halifax Armoury, there was a large crowd from the neighbourhood along with a contingent of reporters. In the dressing room, taping up, the rumour got back to me that Brian Nero had been walking around town, telling people he was going to knock me out in front of my hometown crowd. Taylor sat me down and said, "Okay, look. People have been telling you a lot of shit in here. Now, this guy's nothing but a big kid. You just go in there and do your thing."

Before fight time, I warmed up. My routine was to shadow-box for three minutes, skip rope for three and shadow-box for another three. Taylor would frequently say that the body needed nine minutes of sustained exercise prior to engaging in a fight. His training was rigorous, but it was meant to condition an amateur fighter to fight at full capacity for one round and come back fresh for the next round. Taylor's philosophy was that every round in an amateur fight was to be fought as though it were the first round. In a professional fight, with maybe ten or twelve rounds, there's time to warm up and maybe coast for a round or two. In a three-round amateur match, every round has to be high-intensity.

To be honest, sweating in the dressing room, I came to develop a grudge against Nero. Here was this guy from Toronto, coming into my neighbourhood, walking around on my streets, apparently telling the people in my own community that they were going to see me get knocked out. Some people don't realize that it's better to keep your mouth shut. Bragging about things like that can energize an opponent who might otherwise be more complacent.

I stepped into the ring, and the bell rang. Right off, I caught Nero with a couple of stiff, clean jabs as we circled each other like two caged bears. I knew my hits were solid because I could feel the reverberations of his bones through my gloved-up fingertips. The crowd gasped. I was on my game. My timing was on. My combinations worked. Nero's head started to sag because of the jabs I was landing. With his head cocked like that, he was off balance, and it was difficult for him to cover up. I loaded up and landed a fierce right jab straight to his chin. Nero dropped to the canvas. He wasn't knocked out, but he took a standing eight count and couldn't continue with the fight.

I had stopped Brian Nero in the first round.

I was elated. The Armoury erupted. Once I got over my hesitation about punching Nero, it really wasn't that big of a deal. I just punched him and punched him and punched him again. And I thought to myself, "Okay, now I know I can do this." I'd found my motivation — I didn't like losing. It had been that simple all along.

With my new mindset and the skill set I already had honed, I knew I could compete as a boxer. If I wanted to win, I could do it. I was overjoyed. But in the back of my mind, I couldn't shake a vague sinking feeling. I knew the Halifax police force was figuring out what to do with me next — and that it wouldn't be good.

In Canadian amateur boxing there are individual fights, and then there are regional tournaments. If you win one of the regional tournaments, then you can move on to compete in the next tournament, which covers a bigger geographical region. If you win a regional tournament, you become the champion of that geographic area for one year. Regional championships are determined year in and year out through this tournament system.

Over the course of each tournament, depending on your weight class, you have to fight a number of opponents. If you're a heavyweight, like I was, you might fight three or four people per tournament, depending on the opponents

*Calvin with Dave Singer, coach and trainer, at the Canadian Winter
Games in Lethbridge, Alberta, in 1975.*

you draw. Generally, the heavier weight classes fight fewer
times. Lighter fighters — middleweights, welterweights or
flyweights — might have to fight six or seven opponents
per tournament.

In 1974, I won the Nova Scotia provincial tournament
against a MacDonald from Cape Breton. He was a big,
intimidating man, but he didn't have a lot going for him
in the way of boxing skills. I was able to work my left jab
on him and keep him off balance. I cut his face up in a few
places. It was an unanimous decision in my favour.

Having won the heavyweight regionals in Nova Scotia,
the next tournament on the list for me was the Eastern

Canadian Championships in North Bay, Ontario. That year, our Nova Scotia team consisted of me, Kevin Downey, Chris Clarke, who became a world-class contender, and Ricky Anderson, who also became a world-class champ. Taylor Gordon was our team coach. At twenty-five, I was the elder statesman of this outstanding group of young fighters.

I fought my way through to the finals in the tournament. Rick Petch was my opponent, and he was a methodical fighter. I was a much quicker fighter than he was, but my timing was off. I managed to keep him off of me, and I made him fight my fight. But it wasn't my best work, and I could've fought a lot better than I did. I didn't feel like I'd won, but the judges gave me the victory.

"Just keep quiet," Taylor said. "You got the decision."

And that gave me the 1974 Eastern Canadian heavy-weight title.

Calvin with other Winter Games participants in Lethbridge in 1975.

After that, it was the Canadian Winter Games, which were in Nova Scotia that year. This was the big tournament of the year. I stopped my first opponent in the first round and figured I had a shot at the Canadian title. Then I ran up against a boxer by the name of Bill Turner. Turner was very, very tough and was a very organized fighter — he made no mistakes.

No matter how hard I hit him, it didn't seem to matter. Until then, I'd never fought someone who, even if I hit them as hard as I could, remained unfazed. It was a startling realization. The best I could do was land punches and stay out of his way. Dave Singer, a trainer who worked with Taylor, was in my corner. Between rounds he asked, "What's the matter?"

"Well," I said, "I'm hitting him, and nothing's happening."

As the fight went on, I had to keep moving around Turner. I'd move in, try and land a few punches without getting hurt myself, and then dodge out of his way. There was no hurting the man. I guess all the weaving and ducking and dancing out of his way tired me out, and I fatigued pretty badly. In the third round, he had his way with me. He hit me quite hard quite a few times, and the referee gave me a couple of standing eight counts. I lost the match, and I'd been battered pretty badly in the process.

When I came out of the ring with the loss, I felt decent, but definitely not great. I guess I must have looked a little green, because every second person in the crowd asked me if I wanted to go see a doctor. I made it out of the ring under my own power and managed to get my street clothes back on and stumble out of the arena. But later that night, as I was eating dinner, a filling came out of my mouth; Bill Turner had knocked it loose. I thought, "Damn. This is not good."

I spent the next year focusing on my training. All my fighting, all my training and all my competing — the Provincial Championship, the Eastern Canadian Championship and the Canadian Championship — I did in my spare time. I worked my rotating shifts with the police, the four to midnight, the midnight to eight and the eight to four. During the four-to-midnight shift, when I couldn't train at the gym, I did road work and wind sprints to keep up my aerobic capacity. When I worked the midnight-to-eight and the eight-to-four shifts, I would hit the gym at night. Taylor would run me through calisthenics, sparring, hitting the bags and circuit training.

By now the Nova Scotia sports media were beginning to take notice of my boxing tournaments, and I was getting written up. The Halifax Police Department was still trying to intimidate me into quitting boxing. Reportedly managers were making jokes that the words "Halifax Police Department" should be written on the bottom of my boots for people to see when I got knocked out, lying on the canvas. My boxing on the national stage was bringing prestige to the force, and the best they could do was mock my successes behind my back.

I made my way back to the 1975 Canadian Championships, this time held at the Paul Sauvé Arena in Montreal, Quebec. Once again, the final bout was between me and the force of nature known as Bill Turner. I didn't need to pump myself up for this. Turner had beaten me up the year before, to the point that a filling had fallen out of my mouth. I wanted payback.

Bill had been on my mind for the past year. He had been one of my main sources of motivation. But although I was determined, he had the psychological edge on me. He had already beat me once, resoundingly. And I wasn't really sure I could even hurt him.

At one point early in the first round, he landed a fierce hit on me. I staggered, and for a split second I doubted whether I had what it would take to beat this man. I knew I couldn't take him down, and that I would have to beat him technically by outmanoeuvring him over the span of three rounds. I used my footwork, my left jab and my right hand. I hit him with everything I had. I rocked him with hard rights, and he still kept coming. My conditioning had improved from the year before, and as the fight went on, I basically put him in a boxing glove factory. I punched and punched and weaved out of the way of his reach. I did everything I could to stop him. He didn't go down, but I definitely hurt him. And I definitely won the fight.

As the referee raised my hand in victory, I looked over at Bill and told him not to stop training. In my heart I knew — with my annual leave all used up — that the Halifax Police Department would not let me compete in the upcoming '76 Olympics in Montreal. As the Canadian amateur champ, the spot was supposed to be mine, but I knew that honour would likely fall to Bill instead.

When I got home to Nova Scotia, I put the gold medal around my father's neck. I had come a long way from our sessions in the kitchen, from being bullied daily in the old neighbourhood and from the days when he wasn't sure that I'd ever even stand up for myself. We laughed and cried together, remembering all those lessons around the kitchen table.

Back to work in uniform the next day, I walked into Inspector Leo Storm's office wearing the medal. I counted Storm as one of my policing mentors, but on this day, he had this incredulous look on his face, as though he was privy to some gossip he wanted to share with me but couldn't. He looked at me as though he knew the measure of the storm that was coming.

As the heavyweight representative on Team Canada, the next tournament in which I was supposed to compete was the North American Championships in Miami, Florida. But I had no leave left, and the Halifax police wouldn't budge. They had told me their position all along, but I figured they'd understand that this was a chance to bring prestige and honour to the force, and they would readjust themselves accordingly. But it wasn't to be; they didn't let me compete. So while I was supposed to be the Canadian heavyweight representative in Miami, instead I watched the North American Championships on my television set.

Taylor Gordon was livid. He went down to the station and tore a strip off the chief of police. I'm not sure what was said between them, but shortly after their meeting I was summoned to the chief's office. The inspector who'd originally told me that I was not allowed to compete was there. He had his back turned to me, and he was looking out the window. He couldn't even look at me. Chief of Police Robinson got to the point. He reiterated that the department didn't give time off for sports. I simply acknowledged what he'd said and left his office. I was on track to compete in the Olympics. Sports Canada had designated me a carded athlete, which meant that I would receive funding from the federal government for my training. I had hoped that management at Halifax police would see I wasn't just asking for time off to throw horseshoes, or whatever.

When I told Taylor about my meeting with the chief, he went straight to the Halifax press. The media circus kicked off. A couple of days later, I was asleep at home after a night shift when the phone rang. When I answered, I was live on the local radio. Some host was asking me about not being allowed to compete in the Olympics. I groggily answered a few simple questions, then I got my head together and shut the interview down. Next thing I knew, I was watching Harvey Kirk, the anchorman for CTV national news, reporting on my story, "Police officer not allowed to go to the Olympics."

Then the political manoeuvrings in Halifax got underway. Talk circulated through the police station, and comments began to appear in the press. Suddenly, everyone had an opinion.

"It would be great if Calvin was the first black sergeant in the Halifax Police Department!"

Or, "It would be great if Calvin went to the Olympics! Think of what it would do for the force!"

When this was all being fought out in the press, Leo Storm, then the officer in charge of my platoon, kept telling me, "I told them! I told them!" He had known me for years and seemed to now pride himself on his predictive powers as to what was going to happen between myself and the police force. I guess he'd known for years that this whole thing was headed for a collision, and I remember him constantly saying to me, "Calvin, they're gonna have trouble with you. Aren't they?"

At that time, I didn't know what the hell Leo was talking about. So I just laughed him off. Ultimately though, Storm knew that at the end of the day, I was my own man. In other words, you can ask me to do something for you. You can try and argue with me to do or not do something. But I'll weigh it out for myself and come to my own decisions. You can persuade me with your argument and with your fact-based information. But you can't threaten me, and you certainly can't buy me. My ancestors fought with their lives to break free from slavery. At this point, bowing low and just taking orders is not in my DNA.

A few days later, while doing some shopping at the Scotia Square Mall, I ran into Edmond Morris, the mayor of Halifax. He picked me out of the crowd, approached me and asked what I'd like to do about the whole situation of the police force squashing my dreams of Olympic

Calvin with Leo Storm at Krowell's Drug Store in Halifax in 1972.

Calvin at 2658 Belle Aire Terrace in Halifax in 1973.

competition. I knew that while Chief Robinson had made his decision, the mayor or Gerald Reagan, then the premier of Nova Scotia, could apply political pressure in the proper avenues and overrule Robinson's negative verdict. With my shopping bags in hand, I explained to the mayor that while I did certainly have thoughts on the matter, I could not adequately explain my feelings right there and then in the shopping mall.

Morris replied, "Okay. Well, let's schedule an appointment for you to come and talk to me."

My situation had become an embarrassment to the city because Taylor had gone to the press before the municipal government had had a chance to spin their angle to the media, or even to take up a position on the matter. The story had gone national, and it had caught the mayor and the city off their guard.

A couple days later, I called up the mayor's office to make the appointment. When we spoke, he said, "Calvin, I hope that you'll be man enough to say that we arranged this meeting prior to your story hitting the press."

I replied, "Sure. No problem."

Then, between the time I met the mayor in the mall and the scheduled time of our meeting, another story broke in the press. Suddenly I was reading a heartstring-tugging story about how a black alderman in Halifax had pressured the mayor to organize a meeting with me. Whether this was bullshit or true, I knew now that I was being racially showcased. My boxing career had become a *cause célèbre* for the mayor and the alderman to jockey and score political points in the media.

I went to the alderman, who lived in the community, with the newspaper in my hand and asked him point blank, "What the fuck is this all about?"

He replied, "Well, you know, for the optics of it all, it would look better if the public thought that it went down this way."

Uh-huh. That's pretty much the moment when I decided I wasn't going to participate. I wasn't going to let myself be played as a political pawn, and I wasn't going to watch my story play out in the daily news cycle.

You all don't want me to go to the Olympics?

Fine.

Then you all take the bad publicity. As for me, I'm not going to go beg the local political puppet masters for the chance to represent my city, my community, my police force and my country. I fought fair and square to get there. I'll retire as the Canadian Amateur Heavyweight Champion of 1975. Screw it.

Still, I went to the meeting with the mayor. The black alderman was there in the office. I guess that the look on my face told them where I stood on the matter. The alderman started in, "Calvin, you should still go to the Olympics!"

In the end, I knew that he had my best interest at heart. At the end of the day, we liked and respected each other. But I wasn't going to let myself become politicized in this manner.

I told him, "I'm not going, and that's it. I'm not going to be a pawn in the political process."

I was fed up with the bullshit. The story as I saw it was supposed to be about sporting success, not about my blackness or about politicians looking to win votes and handshakes by championing my cause. At this point, my trust had been broken. I figured that if the Halifax police did capitulate and let me fight in the Olympics, they'd do something behind my back — something to derail my career — that I would have no control over. I'd had enough of the plotting behind my back, and of institutions and people who had nothing to do with me trying to look good at my emotional expense.

The local police association suggested that Halifax police officers could each offer me one day off of their annual leave, so that I could compete. But I didn't want to go compete in the Olympics as some kind of departmental charity case. Besides, some of my co-workers let me know, in no uncertain terms, that they had zero interest in helping me succeed. The fraternity and brotherhood that the association was hoping to highlight and work with was actually non-existent. I wasn't one of the "good ol' boys," and I never would be. I was — and had always been — a black token on the force. As a teen, I had allowed the prestige of the uniform to overwhelm me, but the reality around me was becoming all too painfully clear.

The head of the police association called me up, and I told him of my decision not to fight in the Olympics. I remember him asking me, "What about your obligation to your country?"

I replied, "How is it that I'm not fulfilling my obligation to my country? Every day I put my life on the line by being a police officer!"

Just more fucking politics.

Looking back, in my opinion the Halifax Police Department could have temporarily reorganized my schedule so that I could have trained in the mornings and nights leading up to the Olympics. If they could have worked with me — and understood the opportunity this presented for glory not only for the police force, but also for black communities across Nova Scotia — I wouldn't have had to take any time off work to train for the Olympics. It could have all been sorted out internally without the racial showcasing or the media circus.

On top of that, I think that it could have been a much-needed opportunity for bridge-building between two communities that only months before had been preparing to go to war with each other. Yes, training for the Olympics would have been incredibly intense. Maybe I wouldn't have had enough time to train properly. But I had won the Canadian Championships in my spare time.

As it was, the Canadian Boxing Association didn't send anyone in the heavyweight division to the '76 Olympics in Montreal.

I continued working out and sparring. I became a sparring partner for Trevor Berbick, who went on to fight Muhammad Ali and Mike Tyson, and who at one time was the World Heavyweight Champion. Taylor Gordon kept at me and tried to persuade me to try out for the upcoming Commonwealth Games. But the potential of future political hijinks bore zero interest for me. I would have had to do the whole bitter fight outside the ring all over again just to fight inside the ring. Boxing, for me, had always been my release from anger. Now, increasingly, all the peripheral bullshit that was attaching itself to my boxing was just making me angrier.

I'm not bitter, but these days, when I think back on my amateur boxing career and more generally on my time with the Halifax Police Department, my thoughts turn to the poem "Dream Deferred" by Langston Hughes:

> *What happens to a dream deferred?*
> *Does it dry up*
> *like a raisin in the sun?*
> *Or fester like a sore —*
> *And then run?*

Frankly, it could have been so much more than it was.

In 2012, I was inducted into the Yarmouth, Nova Scotia, Sports Hall of Fame. I donated all my medals, including the 1975 Canadian Championship medal, to the Yarmouth Sports Museum. Taylor Gordon, Sherry Lawrence and Dave Downey were all in attendance — a bunch of old-timers now.

As for my policing career, things for me in Halifax were never quite the same after that. The racial bullshit that surrounded my boxing career had spilled over into my daily policing. It was as though the blinders had come off my eyes, and it was suddenly obvious to me that all of us black police officers had simply been hired as part of the response to the Black Panther Party coming to Halifax. I don't know why it wasn't clearer to me before that. We were all hired solely for that purpose, and with the Panthers gone, no matter how hard we worked, we were not going to be afforded the same opportunities for promotions and assignments as our white colleagues.

I was wearing the uniform to appease the black community. I was like a living, breathing, walking goodwill gesture. But now that the Black Panthers had gone back to the States, it was like, "Okay . . . they're gone. Things can go back to the way they were around here."

With all of the racist behaviour taking place in the force, I wondered whether we black officers were on the chopping block.

When would we be rendered expendable?

Would the force make up some excuse to shuffle us off?

Would we be picked off, one by one?

Would they try to make us so fed up with the way we were being treated that we would leave?

Seven years into my policing career, the truth had become crystal clear.

It takes five to seven years to become a well-rounded police officer, to develop your style and to pick what areas of policing you intend to specialize in if you plan on moving on from general policing. It's around that seven-year mark when promotional eligibility comes into play. Personally, with an eye towards advancement and specialization, I had applied to the traffic division and to the motorcycle division.

My applications were completely ignored.

Why? I don't know.

I applied to the Community Relations section. My application was denied. No explanation was provided.

Eventually, I was given a three-month stint in the Detectives' Office. My day-to-day duties included driving inspectors and superintendents back and forth to their homes for lunch and to their other appointments. I should have worn a bowtie and black leather gloves; I was nothing more than a glorified chauffeur. When serious crimes occurred, my driving duties were put on hold until the crime was investigated. But small investigations took a back seat to my chauffeuring responsibilities. To me, it was a clear message from the force that I was not supposed to thrive as a cop. I was meant to give in and submit or, alternately, become frustrated and lose my cool. I certainly wasn't being groomed for promotional opportunities. Without any options, I opted to go back to street duties, where at least I knew that every shift I worked could potentially replace a racist white cop walking the beat.

Even back on the beat, however, there was a real danger. I had become a very good police officer. I did it in my own way and in my own style, but positive results were the outcome. Over and over again. But the harder I worked and the more competent I became in this toxic environment, the more threatened my co-workers became of my abilities. A token is expected to know its role, not reinvent itself.

My methods were interpreted as outlandish or maverick, rather than forward-thinking and community-based. I was given some latitude to operate my own way. But I was never put in a position where I could develop materials or programs to improve policing in minority neighbourhoods or change the way things were done. At the end of the day, I was still just a nigger in a uniform, and to certain people in positions of power, that would never be acceptable.

Over time, all this bullshit started to take an emotional and psychological toll on me. It went beyond the stress of the work. I was losing my humanity. I saw myself becoming just like my father, a survival unit, getting up every morning and operating to subsist in a hostile work environment. When I looked down the road, career-wise, I saw absolutely nothing. I thought back to my childhood and the emotional difficulties that had tormented my father. Unable to count on my own emotional and mental state, I started to close in on myself. I didn't pursue any serious relationships. I passed on getting married. I couldn't invest the time or mental energy on building a family or having kids. I didn't buy a house or invest in the future. If this was going to be my life, I wasn't going to infect anyone else with it.

I remember Leo Storm telling me that if I played my cards right, I could make it to inspector.

I'd say, "Yeah, yeah. That's great."

I knew what he meant. He meant that if I just behaved myself like a good Uncle Tom, I'd be groomed and placed on a pedestal — racially showcased, that is. I'd be "The one! The best! The brightest! The only!"

Black police officers absolutely must know the rules of this game going in. They have to know that, despite their best efforts, they will not overturn the deep structural racism that characterizes policing forces. They can expect to be used as black faces in the right places. Their skills as police officers may not be the prime determinant in how their careers in law enforcement play out.

They must know that for every black officer being showcased as "the chosen one," there are dozens of black cops whose accomplishments are being downplayed daily. Black police officers who are promoted must not allow themselves to become the black face of racist behaviour.

Don't get me wrong. Politics always takes precedence over performance in the promotion system of policing. And this isn't limited to the barriers applied to black officers. But politics over performance as the golden rule rings especially true when black police officers enter the mix. Black police officers are first compared to each other, and then their value is weighed in terms of how they can serve the police organization from a racial perspective.

Will they be racially tailored? Or racially showcased?

Lost in the force's assessment are important questions, such as:

What if the black person being hired doesn't actually want to be involved in policing their own community?

What if they don't want to be tokens meant to defuse a conflict between the black community and the police?

What if they aspire to become a multi-dimensional police officer with an actual career, judged on their merits, with the possibility for advancement, just like a white officer?

My community was right, black officers are expected to be good "white man's niggers."

There are always exceptions to the rule. But make no mistake, that is the rule.

I can't explain the effect that this dawning awareness had on me. I had been played, and now I was trapped, as far as my policing career was concerned. For a time, I did the bare minimum in my duties. I was clinically depressed and began to engage in self-destructive behaviour. Looking back, I was hurting myself before others had the chance to do it. I neglected my health. I didn't care how I treated myself. I began to harbour a great deal of resentment and anger. I was in a constant state of inner turmoil, and even the punching bag didn't ease my mind anymore.

I came to empathize with the collective anger, always verging on rage, that slow-boiled through the streets of my own community. I did not condone — but I understood

— why some black people had turned to lives of crime. Around me, I watched white police officers who couldn't carry my handcuffs move up the promotional ladder. Always somebody's son. Or somebody's cousin. Or somebody's friend of a friend. Halifax was a small and a white place, and we black officers were living the assimilation fantasy. And as with all fantasies, there was supposed to be a happy ending where everyone lived happily ever after.

If I just worked hard and waited, then success would come.

Wait and believe!

But hold on, here's the actual reality — the first black police officer, Layton Johnson, was hired in 1967. He was gone within two years. The first black officer promoted was Max Hartley, in 1995. Max was hired with me, in 1969. Throughout his career, Max refused to be racially show-cased. When the press came calling, in 1995, to make a big splash about his being the first black police officer to be promoted, he gave them the cold shoulder. And Max was the only black officer promoted in the history of the Halifax Police Department prior to amalgamation in 1996. So tell me, in twenty-eight years, were there no other black police officers eligible for promotion?

But no. Just wait and believe.

Yet still, I had white officers telling me to my face, after seven years, "Calvin, you want to be promoted, but you just won't wait."

Wait.

Wait for what?

I wouldn't wait.

I made plans to leave the Halifax Police Department (renamed Halifax Regional Police in 1996) for the RCMP. I had no illusions that the RCMP was going to be any kind of different experience. I knew that the RCMP, from its very inception, was an instrument of white supremacy. But I assumed the holes in the net of racist behaviour would be a bit bigger, and that there might be opportunities for career advancement in the organization. I was going to trade my community for a chance at a career. I knew I'd have to leave Halifax, and probably Nova Scotia, for the possibility of meaningful employment in law enforcement in Canada.

Blair Jackson, a sergeant on my platoon who later became chief of police in Halifax, told me, "If you stay, I'll fight for you."

I thought to myself, "*Stay.* Stay for what? Stay to wait?"

"*Fight for me.* What the fuck does that actually mean?"

"Doesn't my record as a police officer speak for itself? Doesn't my record fight for me? Why would *you* have to *fight* for *me*? And who, actually, is it that you are fighting against?"

Enough!

CHAPTER 5
PAIN AND PLEASURE OF A NEW START

Any officer, upon leaving the Halifax Police Department, usually had what was referred to as a "smoker." This was a party thrown in the departing officer's honour. There was drinking, food and general revelry. A smoker was also a symbolic event. It was an acknowledgement by the force that they were marking the loss of a good cop, someone who would be missed by their co-workers. Some members, upon leaving the force, also were presented with their police badge, framed and mounted. A memento of their service. A token of their contribution.

Nobody organized a smoker for me. To be clear, I didn't want a smoker just for the sake of having folks throw me a party. I wanted to say a proper goodbye to the people I had worked with and had come to respect. Also, smokers were organized by fellow police officers, so I guess this was just another indication that I was not part of the rank and file — according to the rank and file themselves. Instead, I just cleaned out my locker by myself and left the building.

It was 1977, and I was twenty-eight years old.

I had been a police officer with the department for a full eight years with no promotions, and every opportunity for advancement seemingly blocked. Eight years earlier, I had been standing on the corner with Ricky Smith just shooting the dozens. Eight years earlier, as an awestruck teenager, with the threat of the Black Panthers in the air, I had met with Chief Mitchell and had been given a summer job. The Halifax police was where I had become whatever kind of policeman — and man — I was going to be.

Racist behaviour, politics, nepotism and conflicts aside, I'd made friends in the Halifax Police Department, and I had done a lot of good work. And it was sad to go out this way. Through my professionalism and my deportment, I had built bridges between the police and the black community.

I left the Halifax Police Department as an angry man — the man I'd sworn that I wouldn't become. White supremacy had planted its seed, and now the kernel of self-destruction was growing inside of me. I was a man that some in the force would sooner bathe in the "Nigger Bath" than ride side-by-side with on motorbike patrol. Within me now grew bitter layers of disappointment — at being used as a token; at losing friends, mentors, personal relationships and family; at having gained a brutal first-hand education in the realities of racist behaviour; and now at the long shadow cast over the opportunities I'd desired for a better career and life.

I always believed that I could — and should — have been promoted to a leadership position within the force. My ideas, if maximized, would have enhanced the relation-ship between the Halifax police and the black community. I could have bridged the gap between the two warring camps by implementing organized interactions on a large scale.

Under my watch, I could have at least doubled the opportunities for interactions between the police and the black community.

Given the chance, I would have had black community members address all new recruits to the force. I would have had community members talk about the history of policing as it applied to the black community. I would have had them talk about episodes of police violence that took place against black folks — for example, the beating of Ronald Drummond, a black prisoner, by a Halifax police officer — and the responses that these triggered in the black community and the impacts they had on the community. I would have had black community members share their views on what constituted good policing.

At the end of their basic training, I would have arranged a dialogue between new recruits and the black community, facilitated by seasoned police officers. Conversely, I would have explained in detail to the black community why the police do what they do. I would have explained in detail to the recruits how the black community had come to hate the police.

I wanted the police educated on the history of the black community. I wanted growth for both sides. And that would have been achieved if my plan had become a standard component of basic training for new recruits. My approach would only have been limited by the imagination of the community and the police force. Instead, I'd lost it all. I was still young, with a chance to start again, but I never would have left Halifax if I'd seen even the smallest chance for meaningful advancement. Everything was gone to me but my dedication to the principles of law enforcement.

In the RCMP interview, in their office in Halifax, I was

put through a battery of questions. The first was, "So, tell me the story about what happened with your boxing."

Clearly there was some concern — and interest — about hiring me. I had openly and publicly challenged the local white power structure. White people in power don't forget that.

I explained to the interview committee that I'd been repeatedly told by management at Halifax police that I wasn't allowed to box, when there was no actual policy that prohibited me from doing it. I explained that my actions in the boxing ring had never been detrimental to the Halifax Police Department. That, actually, they had been a benefit. With every one of my boxing victories, accolades and congratulations had come in from international and national bodies, from policing organizations and individuals from around the world, congratulating me on the fact that I was a police officer taking part in high-level amateur boxing. These letters of respect were not only addressed to me; many were sent to my superiors on the force.

I explained that I had won the Canadian amateur heavyweight championship in my spare time, and that I had never missed a minute of work for training or fighting, or due to injury.

I obviously explained myself to their satisfaction because I soon got a letter stating that I had been accepted into RCMP training.

Oddly enough, a few days after the letter arrived in the mail, I received a phone call from the RCMP telling me I was going to be posted to Newfoundland, and asking, "Do you still want to join?"

"Yes," I replied.

It wasn't common practice for the RCMP to assign

someone to a post prior to the completion of basic training. Personally, I thought Newfoundland was an odd posting, as isolated as it was. In my initial interview, the committee had noted that I'd done quality work to lessen the conflict between the black community and the police in Halifax. I'd assumed that the RCMP's most logical move would be to keep me in Nova Scotia, particularly in some kind of community-relations capacity.

The RCMP knew I had ties to the black community. They knew I had worked in the black community, and that I had a good record. My police work in general, aside from the racial issues which plagued me, was well known and respected. In my mind, there were positions I could have taken with the RCMP in Nova Scotia that would have used my unique skill sets to the force's advantage. I didn't know whether I had drawn the interest of particular bureaucrats in the RCMP, or whether I had upset powerful players in the province, but it was Newfoundland for me — one of the most isolated areas in Canada. Without a black community of any size, in a certain sense it was like being banished.

Still, I said yes. At this point, what else could I have done?

In 1977, I reported to the RCMP Depot in Regina, Saskatchewan. New recruits usually spend six months in training. In my case, I was assigned to a troop of recruits who had previous policing experience, so we had a modified, three-month program that built on our pre-existing skills and knowledge. Three other Halifax police officers who'd left the force at the same time as me were in my troop. I guess there was a minor exodus going on from the Halifax police at the time, and I was happy to see some friendly faces in the unfamiliarity of a Regina barracks. Curt Taylor, who was also in my recruitment class with the Halifax Police Department

Calvin's RCMP graduation photo, taken in Regina, Saskatchewan, in 1978.

in 1969, was there with me. We still keep in touch.

The training itself consisted of policing sciences, which comprises learning the Canadian *Criminal Code*, federal statutes and force policy. The skills units included driving, firearms training, self-defence, drills, deportment and swimming. I didn't have any trouble with these skills; we seasoned recruits had already learned much of what we were being taught in our respective police training.

What I found fascinating — and troubling — was the quasi-military approach the RCMP trainers took with the new recruits. We stayed in barracks. We were issued articles from a kit that had to be displayed, used and returned to their place exactly as found. We marched wherever we went. And if we weren't marching, we were running. We wore brown coveralls and police boots. It became apparent, quite quickly, that the months at Depot were an indoctrination process, plain and simple.

This type of training process removed young, impressionable recruits — many straight out of high school and with no policing experience — from their families, friends and homes, and introduced a new routine that included different foods, dorm living, an absence of privacy, a lack of sleep, rigidly timed schedules and a new technical language, all while wearing uniforms that marked a separation between the in-crowd of recruits and the general populace-at-large. As a police officer with an eye towards community relations, the sharp distinction being taught — that of a break between those in uniform and those without — immediately set off my internal alarm bells.

I saw our collective isolation from the familiar and the intended destruction of our former life patterns, followed by a mental and psychological rebuilding process in which new values were instilled and rewarded, as the same standard of indoctrination that was used upon children in Canada's residential schools, military recruits in the United States Marines and other units and devotees of religious fringe groups and cults. In my case, it was meant to break down my individuality and rebuild me in the image of an RCMP officer — strong, firm, committed to justice and blindly obedient to authority.

This went far beyond a standard education process.

On its own, strict adherence to order and obedience isn't a bad idea. In fact, obedience is necessary in a paramilitary organization. For certain individuals, building a degree of obedience into the education process may in fact be quite beneficial. Obedience becomes a bad idea when you teach impressionable recruits, with zero policing experience, that there is no flexibility in policing practices. In policing, thinking outside the box is vital. It means changing and adapting your tactics and strategies to fit volatile situations, in response to the actual fast pace of the real world. Adaptive strategizing might save your life, the life of your partner or the lives of those you are charged with protecting. Confining recruits to command-and-control environments and teaching this style of blind obedience restricts their thinking.

It also troubled me that new recruits were taught only the positive aspects of the RCMP in Canadian history. As a young man, I knew very little of the RCMP's checkered past. But I knew we weren't the superheroes we were being taught to be.

In Regina, the red serge was akin to a priest's cassock. It was holy garb, unstained and perfect. There was no mention of the shame of the RCMP tearing First Nations children away from their families and placing them in residential schools, the blind obedience of following orders or the institution's history of racism so well documented in Craig Smith's book *You Had Better Be White by Six A.M.*

Just as an example, the suppression of the 1885 Red River Rebellion was held up as a moment of organizational pride. When I arrived in Regina as a new recruit, a piece of the rope used to hang Louis Riel was on display, behind glass, as though it was a religious icon. It was as if the force's role in suppressing Riel's attempt to have Métis land claims acknowledged — and then subsequently hanging him — was a point of pride, something to celebrate as a victory rather than a dark stain on the past.

Away from home, isolated from the outside world, the RCMP propaganda machine worked the image of the glorious red serge into impressionable young minds twenty-four hours a day, seven days a week. The superhuman, almost mythical aura of the RCMP officer permeated the process, which was never tempered with reality. Graduating cadets would wear t-shirts with images of Mounties rough-riding a buffalo, smashing through brick walls. We were being taught that we were invincible — and always correct.

For new recruits, the red serge was everything. Wearing it, they became larger than life — icons or caricatures in their own minds. I looked around and asked myself, "What will these people actually think they're doing when they go out and patrol the streets? Will they approach policing as though they're superhuman? Will they actually believe they're godlike? How will they possibly perceive themselves as responsible to — and part of — the communities they will serve?"

My fellow troop mates, with prior policing knowledge under their belts, did not buy in to this approach. We were all experienced police officers, and we'd each developed our own policing styles. But we went through the motions. Because we were in the modified training program, my troop wore the brown fatigues of new recruits on one day, and red serge the next. The new recruits, on the other hand, were on a progressive training regimen, meaning it was several weeks of brown fatigues before they graduated to being allowed to wear the red serge. Seeing themselves in uniform for the first time sometimes went to their heads and gave them an inflated sense of their own importance.

When new recruits in their red serge, preening like peacocks, saw us seasoned officers in our fatigues, they'd try to order us around. Despite our years of policing, seeing us in brown, they felt that they'd earned this particular privilege. Some of the braver ones would get up in our faces and bark orders at us, while their peer group surrounded and supported them. This led to some very interesting confrontations with some of the mouthier cadets.

We were all grown men, and we tried to be understanding with these young pups. And we did have to go along with the Depot protocols, to a degree. But when they got abusive or outright aggressive in their comments, then the kids were slam-dunked back into their place. We were police veterans, not the targets of abuse for kids in red serge, away from home for the first time and feeling self-important.

I never bought in to the glory of the red serge or the attendant propaganda and philosophy. That kind of misplaced faith was never for me. My dedication was to being a police officer. What that meant to me, fundamentally, was serving my community — wherever I might find myself. It never occurred to me to remove myself from my community, or be apart from my community; in fact, a separation like that would be counter to the process of policing my community.

It didn't matter what force I worked for, or whether the uniform was red serge or plain navy blue. I suspect there are recruits, however, who I trained with and who have since retired, who are eating off of RCMP-logo dishes with RCMP-logo cutlery, and have their red serge uniforms displayed on mannequins in their basements. Others I know have become members of various RCMP veterans' associations and will die working for RCMP causes. It's so easy to fall in love with the uniform and not the process, and I am not criticizing them for that. But in my opinion, there is much more to life than dying in the hallway on your way home, drunk, from an RCMP mess.

During training, I saw alcohol abuse introduced as an integral component of the RCMP's indoctrination process. Starting in training, and continuing throughout their careers, new members were expected to conform to the higher-ranking members' agendas. And, at certain times, this involved episodes of binge drinking.

From my years in the Halifax Police Department, I was used to a culture of alcohol consumption, which sometimes crossed the line into alcohol abuse. The difference with the RCMP was that, right from the first day of training, subsidized alcohol was readily promoted and available to recruits.

This wasn't a question of meeting for drinks after work to unwind after a hard day at the office. The Depot in Regina had five drinking establishments — the Stand Easy Lounge (for cadets only), the Corporals' Mess, the Sergeants' Mess, the Officers' Mess and the Drill Hall on base, where alcohol was also served whenever there was a social function. Rather than having a couple of drinks after shift to socialize, alcohol abuse was a rite of passage, from day one, within RCMP culture.

At the cadets' halfway parties — at the three-month mark of training — instructors were expected to sign a release form in which they assumed legal responsibility for the recruits under their watch. The expectation was that these parties would be drunken blowouts where members-in-training would absolutely lose their senses and get blackout drunk. In fact, the release forms instructors were asked to sign seemed to indicate this was institutionally encouraged. Facilitators and instructors were tasked with putting their wasted recruits to bed. Being a non-drinker, I know from personal experience that any attempt to break with this culture of alcoholism resulted in being labelled uptight, a prude or a teetotaller, and being viewed with suspicion.

After a lifetime of service, I can tell you that alcohol abuse in the RCMP isn't limited to the recruitment stage. This is only the introduction, where young, impressionable minds get formed. Once graduated, RCMP members continue to have ready access to cheap, subsidized booze. Each division or detachment across Canada has a mess, where cheap booze is readily available. And at all the meetings I've ever attended for veteran members of the RCMP, "bar opens at . . ." is a key piece of information never left off the program.

Joseph F. Dietrich, one of the foremost authorities in the world on alcoholism among police, founded the Member Assistance Program in the RCMP. Years later, as a Member Assistance Program member myself, I helped fellow members obtain whatever professional assistance they might require. Without a doubt, the majority of members that sought my assistance were dealing with alcohol or alcohol-related issues.

In 1989, Dietrich conducted a survey of RCMP members, in conjunction with the Clarke Institute (now the Centre for Addiction and Mental Health, or CAMH) in Toronto. Of the 3,500 members across Canada who were sent questionnaires, 3,043 responded. Dietrich's survey found that:

- 11 per cent of members were having seven or more drinks a day.

- 17 per cent of members were having five or more drinks a day.
- 35 per cent of members were having three or more drinks a day.
- 26 per cent of members were in need of psychological intervention.

Dr. Dietrich recommended that the force stop subsidizing alcohol in the messes and actively publicize the results of the survey to highlight the severity of alcohol abuse among RCMP members. Perhaps fearing a tarnished organizational reputation, the RCMP did not release the above information to the public for a significant period of time, and then only after the results were watered down. Ultimately, Dr. Dietrich published his work in 1989 in a study entitled "The Prevalence of Alcohol and Prescription and Over-the-Counter Drug Use in the RCMP."

Given the rates of alcoholism in the force, Dr. Dietrich noted that, statistically, most members would serve under an alcoholic supervisor during the first five years of their service. I can certainly attest to that. To current and former members of the force, I ask you:

During your career did you ever serve at a detachment whose dynamics mirrored those of an alcoholic dysfunctional family?

Did you find yourself and those around you playing out typecast roles which are typically associated with dysfunctional alcoholic families?

Can you remember acting out any — or many — of these roles:

Alcoholic Dependent Person — perfectionist, aggressive, charming, blaming
Chief Enabler — sickly, powerless, compliant, manipulative
Family Hero — successful, independent, seeking approval, perceptive
Scapegoat — sullen, defiant, acting out, blaming
Lost Child — creative loner, solitary, withdrawn
Mascot — hyperactive humourist, centre of attention

To current and former members of the RCMP — and members of dysfunctional families in general — I also ask:

What happens to a family member who criticizes the "family"?

The answer is that the family closes ranks and ostracizes that family member.

To survive, I had to adjust to the dysfunctional RCMP "family." It was, sadly, part of the job. In Regina — with a ticket to a lonely detachment in Newfoundland awaiting me upon graduation — I had nowhere else to go. I worked within the system. I saluted at the right places. And I tucked the corners of my bedsheet just so. Despite the propaganda all around me, upon graduation I was still proud to be an RCMP officer. But I was no more or less proud than I had been to be a police officer in Halifax.

I graduated from the RCMP Training Academy in the early winter of 1978, in the cold and dark of the Canadian prairies. My itinerary had been set for me months before, and I went straight from graduation to the Holyrood detachment in Newfoundland, an hour's drive outside of the provincial capital of St. John's.

Arriving in St. John's on a red-eye flight, I was met at

the airport in the middle of the night and driven to the Holyrood barracks, such as they were. In the last four months, I'd gone from my downtown apartment in Halifax to a barracks in Regina, now to a cot in a room full of used tires, in midwinter, in rural Newfoundland. The next morning, I was introduced to the detachment in Holyrood. When I walked through the door, the looks on my new co-workers faces suggested that nobody had informed them that I was a black man.

In hindsight, Holyrood being a small, rural community on an isolated island in the middle of the Atlantic Ocean, I was probably the first black man that many of them had ever actually seen. Jaws collectively dropped. But the mood was not "Nobody wants you here, nigger." Rather, it was one of surprise, something along the lines of "Wow! Look! A real live black guy!" At various points in my life, I've gotten that look, and ultimately it's one I've learned to live with. At least here I could smell the salt water–tinged air again, which brought reassuring memories of home with it.

Work-wise, while on three-month probation, I settled in. I found that the biggest difference between the Holyrood detachment and my urban policing experience in Halifax was the level of supervision afforded us. In Holyrood, with only thirteen of us in the entire detachment, each officer was expected to know a wide range of duties and to be a self-sufficient law enforcer. Rather than a vertical chain of command, things out in Holyrood operated on a more horizontal basis. It was an excellent work — and learning — environment.

RCMP members in small detachments, without quick access to the specialized departments available in the big cities, do much of their own detective work. And the smaller the detachment, the less specialization and the more experience that individual officers will receive in various aspects of policing. In Halifax, in comparison, beat cops were restricted duty-wise. My people skills and abilities in community policing were well refined, but I'd never been given the opportunity to do much else.

In Halifax, any calls that we officers received while on the beat, whether for break and enters, thefts or other similar crimes, were taken out of our hands and passed on to the Detectives' Office. So while I understood the rules of evidence and investigative techniques, and I knew how to interview suspects and conduct searches, I hadn't had the chance to actually apply these skills. As the months wore on, my co-workers in Holyrood showed themselves to be crack investigators and police officers. And I found myself learning a great deal of policing skills.

Racism in Newfoundland, as I experienced it, presented itself differently than in Halifax. On duty and off, people would call me all kinds of names. Some of the locals would tell me that they "hated" black people. As opposed to Halifax, however, it seemed that their words were just an assumption on their part, something they were supposed to say, rather than something the locals truly felt. To me, their words didn't have that bitter edge of white supremacist behaviour behind their usage. Out here, in the country, far away from everything, there was less to protect — and thus less to restrict me, as a black man, access to.

Whenever somebody told me that they hated black people, I would come back with, "Hey. You've never even seen a black person before, so how do you know you hate me?" And the looks on their faces said, "Hmm. I never expected that answer."

I will say, however, that a significant number of Newfoundlanders did not like to see outsiders, who they refer to as "come-from-aways," in positions of authority. And there was no hiding the fact that I was an outsider. I was the only black cop in Newfoundland. In that rural setting, on call and living in an all-white rural community, I experienced a complete lack of anonymity. I became something of a sideshow — the black Mountie from Holyrood. And being a black cop, with a certain level of authority attached to the position, I become a lightning rod for belligerent racism.

Life in Newfoundland was hard for me at first. I missed my family desperately. I missed the neighbourhoods and alleyways, the claptrap gyms and familiarity of lifelong friends of Halifax. If given the chance, I would rather have stayed with the Halifax Police Department and watched my career blossom. I would rather have participated in the '76 Olympics and made my country, my family and my police force proud.

Holyrood was all right. My co-workers were respectful and we were a family in a way that only a close-knit bunch of rural cops can understand. Over the years, I've maintained meaningful friendships with them. But there was always an impermanence to the entire situation. I was a black man from the big city, and I knew I would never settle there.

Over the years, as I became an experienced officer, as I moved around the country and was posted and reposted, I came to accept my fate as a journeyman cop. Starting all over, introducing myself to a room full of strangers, became easier the more I repeated it. My personal skills and my outward affability served me well in this regard.

Each time, however, as I packed up and moved on, as I took down whatever mementos and tokens I had tacked to the walls of whatever bachelor apartment I had found myself in, the original dream of serving my community in a meaningful manner resurfaced, however briefly, and always more distant on the horizon. I came to understand that there would be no triumphant return to Halifax or Nova Scotia for me. I would visit and walk the streets, and it would always be home. But it would only be the commitment to the job, rather than the place, that would keep me afloat.

Personal goals, like having a family of my own, eluded me. Now, as an old man with some money but no sons or daughters of my own to watch grow, that is a regret and a sadness that stays with me. What was behind my inability to craft and maintain fulfilling personal relationships, I don't know. I don't have the answer. But the decades I spent in youthful anger had made me emotionally numb as a man. As in boxing, my feelings are covered in calluses and emotional scars. Now, attempting to remember those long-ago days, trying to paint you a fuller picture of how I felt, I run into blocks and walls where I should be able to access memories, either fond or painful.

Perhaps in learning to expect racial slurs and taunts from anyone, at any time, I became so guarded that I lost the way back to my core self. Despite my best efforts, I think I've become like my father in this regard — fortified and withdrawn to the point that the walls are my only reference point. Constantly surveying my exterior environment for threats.

Living like an animal.

Not too long ago, one mistake, one false accusation, could get a black man lynched and his balls cut off. Today, one missed judgment from a white police supervisor could mean a ruined career for a black police officer, and a beating — even death — for a black citizen. Add a rampant culture of alcohol abuse into a racist policing framework, and you have a near-perfect storm.

Dr. Dietrich's observations unfortunately held true, even in distant Newfoundland. My first supervisor in Holyrood was an alcoholic. Even though he functioned at a high level and was a decent person, when you have an alcohol-fueled supervisor, you can never relax. There were mood swings, ups and downs that were in no way related to anything predictable. At times, it was tense working with him. Like any dysfunctional alcoholic family, we all had to conform to the highest-ranking member's ideas and values. We formed our alliances and took on our dysfunctional familial roles.

I didn't drink. So I became the enabler.

There used to be drinking sessions in the back room. The detachment staff was sometimes drunk and frequently hung-over. I was the one who smiled in their faces and laughed at their jokes and drove them all home when the last bottle was drunk.

Compared to the things I would later see in the RCMP as my travels took me further and further down the road, the backroom drinking sessions in Holyrood were nothing at all — cute by comparison. In a small community, with a thirteen-person detachment, police officers are closely scrutinized by the people they're serving and protecting. There's no room for public displays of inebriation, or for officers driving around impaired. In a small community, officers have to keep their drinking covert, and my co-workers picked their moments and held their liquor well. Drinking was done away from the public eye. But make no mistake, it was done.

If you look at me with disdain for this, what would you have done?

Turn them all in?

Call the cops?

CHAPTER 6
UNDERCOVER OPERATIONS

One thing I didn't know about RCMP culture was that black members will either be asked to do undercover drug work or can expect to be transferred to a drug section at some point during their careers. Why this is, I don't know, but every black officer that I've ever spent time with has confirmed the experience. I was to be no exception.

The difference between me and a wide-eyed recruit was that I had eight years of experience with the Halifax police. So when I got the call from management asking if I'd like to try my hand at drug work, I wasn't naïve to the processes behind the request. I didn't think that I was something special, or that my policing style stood out, or that I had caught the eye of my superiors with my work ethic. Rather, I was suspicious of the organization's motives. I'd been bitten enough times to wonder what the catch was.

That being said, it didn't dawn on me that I was being culturally pigeonholed. I had never before equated being black with having a "nose for drugs" or having some kind of natural-born ability to procure drugs. I didn't equate being black with being a drug user or a drug dealer. Nor did I understand why it was assumed I would have some kind of natural affinity with other black people who happened to be drug dealers or users. Let's just say that the stupidity of white supremacist ideology never ceases to amaze me.

At the time, I also had no idea how doing drug work can destroy a police officer's career. So when I got my call, although I was cynical, I also thought that it might be a ticket out of Holyrood, where I was beginning to tire of the rural environment, and the shtick of being Newfoundland's token black cop was wearing me thin. I needed some cityscape back in my life, so I said, "Sure. Okay. I'll go undercover and buy some drugs. It sounds like a challenge."

I was sent to Halifax to do an in-person interview with a couple of members from the national drug section. These were the cops who selected undercover operators. Personally, I thought the whole interview process was shabby. After we introduced ourselves, I was run through a series of hypothetical role-playing scenarios, which in my mind had zero to do with the actual purchase of drugs. The interview team sat behind a desk while I sat across from them. They said stuff like, "Okay, Calvin, what would you say if this happened?" and "What would you do if that happened?"

I thought to myself, "Don't ask me what I'd do if this or that happened, then have me explain myself to you. Let's just do it. Let's run an actual scenario, out on the street, so that I can move around."

I had a lifetime of experience hanging out in clubs and walking the streets, talking to everyone and anyone. Sitting in an office trying to describe street scenarios to two detectives

Calvin performing undercover work for the RCMP in 1980.

made no sense to me. And while I'd never purchased drugs, I'd been in more clubs sober than most people will in their lives. I'd interacted with enough criminals to know how to talk like a criminal. I also knew enough to know that real drugs weren't bought from two cops in conservative suits and ties, sitting at a desk. But there was nothing I could say or impart to these guys that had anything to do with my ability to gain the trust of a dealer and make a purchase. I knew

I could read the streets and work the clubs — wherever they put me — and get drugs.

The interview continued, and these guys started questioning my ability to do undercover work simply because I didn't drink alcohol. Remember, this was the late 1970s, when the more outrageous and offbeat you were, the better undercover operator you supposedly made. Drink it up! Live it up. The whole methodology was to convince the criminals you couldn't possibly be a cop, because would a cop *do this crazy shit?*

In my mind, the out-of-control bullshit act might have worked on television, or right up until the moment you had to go to court and take the stand. But under cross-examination, in the hands of a good defence attorney, you actually had to answer for your behaviour. And that's when everything stopped running like your favourite cop show. Because there are three ways that a drug charge can be beat, and one of those is the credibility of the witness. The other ways are continuity of the evidence and identification of the accused. And those three things have to line up to get a conviction. If any one of those are a little shaky, the charge gets tossed.

So if I'm doing undercover work, I can't actually take drugs to buy drugs. I can simulate that I'm nicely buzzed, but if I actually do drugs on the job, then my credibility as a witness is shot. Because how can I swear on the stand, in a cross-examination, that my testimony is verifiable if I was high or drunk at the time? In real-life legal situations, I'd actually blow the whole charge. But back in the seventies, it seemed that the more ethically and morally out of control you were, the more the response from the RCMP headquarters in Ottawa was, "Oh shit, this guy is really good! This guy is undercover operator material."

At the end of my interview, one of the sergeants, a man who had a reputation for doing good undercover work, looked at me and said, "You can't do it."

I just stared at him.

He eased back into his chair and said, "Calvin, you're a nigger and I'm a wop and that's the way it is. We take the misfits from Regina to do the undercover work. And you don't differ from the norm."

I was taken aback. My only thought was, "Aha. And there it is. It took a year and a half before somebody in management called me a nigger in an official RCMP interview. But there it is."

This wasn't the one-stoplight streets of Holyrood, or a drunken bar in St. John's, or even a cadet in red serge trying on the word "nigger" for the first time at Depot in Regina. This was a management-level cop in a position of authority. This cop had the potential to stifle my career opportunities.

If I unpack this particular exchange with the benefit of decades of experience, I see a guy in management who just wants to get his rocks off and call me a nigger. But if he does it outright, without context, he might get in trouble. So he calls himself a wop, to denigrate his own Italian heritage, to get to me. Then and only then does he say what's on his mind, that I'm a nigger. His partner is sitting right there with him in the interview room, and he'll swear it was all just meant to be a joke. If I say otherwise, I'm just a black man with a chip on my shoulder, someone who should just learn to lighten up and take a joke. Chill out, nigger!

I headed back to Newfoundland, rejected from the national undercover course. The thing was, at that time there were actually no strict criteria for doing undercover work. You didn't need to have completed the national course to do the work. So with the front door locked, I slipped on in the back door.

Word travelled fast within the police community on our sparsely populated island, and a corporal in the drug section in Corner Brook, a small city on the west coast of Newfoundland, heard that I was interested in doing under-cover work. He gave me a call and suggested I come on over to the west coast and try my hand at undercover work by making small-time drug busts. I figured, why not?

Soon enough, I was dressed up in my finest seventies black drug dealer get-up. I let my hair grow out and donned my wool-lined jean jacket. My crew and I patrolled everywhere from Saint Anthony to Stephenville. We hit up these tiny Newfoundland outports and little fishing villages all up and down the coast. I was the buyer, and I just used my gut instinct, honed by my years of walking the beat. I'd coolly wander around the towns, find somebody hang-ing out, and size them up from a distance. According to a 1971 study by University of California professor Albert Mehrabian, body language is 60 per cent of communica-tion, and I could generally spot a drug dealer, or user simply by the way they carried themselves. I didn't even need to say or hear a word to know. I would approach them in the crowd, and nine times out of ten, I was right. More likely than not, if they didn't sell drugs, they knew somebody who did.

I used my colour like a costume. I was a black man, just looking to score. And *of course*, as RCMP headquarters knew, a black man uses drugs. Almost without exception, these users would run off to their dealers and get me some drugs. It was as easy as that. At this point, it was nothing big, just matchboxes of hashish and different amounts of marijuana.

I'd buy the drugs, make notes and later give evidence. There were no wiretaps and no surveillance. It was just me making my cold calls to small-time dealers I'd never seen before in my life. And likely never would again. That was basically the extent of it, at first.

Personally, I knew that this hot streak of small-time busts would be short-lived; the same thing that initially made me beyond suspicion — my blackness — ensured that my presence would be remembered in every one of these communities. My colour was my prop. And once you blow your prop, it's like the magician revealing the trick behind an illusion. The show's over, and the deception is laid bare for what it is. Calvin the Newfoundland outport drug buyer was a limited-run performance.

That being said, I was pretty good at it. Had I gotten into undercover drug work off the bat, before I started working my regular duties in uniform in Holyrood, I could have busted a whole lot more people. As it was, a few miles outside of Holyrood, somebody sitting across from me at the local bar looked at me sideways and said, "Hey. Aren't you the black guy that works in Holyrood?"

I sipped my Coke and said, "Not me. You got the wrong guy."

He stared hard. Too hard. Finally he said, "Man you got a twin or something, 'cuz you look just like him."

This interaction took place in Gander, Newfoundland, and I knew then that I couldn't continue my undercover act. I had bought my last matchbox of Newfie hash, and we wrapped up the mission. On the whole, the road trip was considered a success. After my tour of rural Newfoundland, I was re-interviewed by two different officers from the national drug section in Ottawa. They determined that I could indeed buy drugs, despite my sobriety, and that I was eligible to take the undercover operators course.

The course itself was held in Vancouver, British Columbia. I can't divulge a lot about the techniques we were taught because they're still being taught, and giving too many secrets away might endanger active members who are working undercover at the moment. But generally, the course provided us with the ideas and mechanisms that were meant to help in undercover work.

Learning to be undercover operators, we were put through a variety of exercises. We learned how to start up conversations in bars and how to walk that fine line between awkward silence and annoyingly sociable. Basically, the instructors were trying to teach me charisma.

We were also taught how to live out on the streets, to stay alive and survive without any outside contact and without money, for extended periods of time. We were taught that while you were out on an undercover mission, you could do anything to get by, except commit crimes.

We were also tested to see how controllable we were as operators. For example, if we were in the middle of a drug-buy scenario and our cover person said, "Let's go. Now," then we had to go, regardless of what was going on, or how long we'd been working on the buy. The controller's word was final. If you resisted or didn't listen in any way, you'd be placing your teammates' lives at risk. And they wouldn't take a chance with you on the streets.

Blind obedience? This was a time it came in handy.

We also learned how to be a cover person. This wasn't like the movies, where an undercover operator does their own thing, goes solo, gets the drugs, busts the dealers and comes back after an extended mission, although that has happened on occasion. For the most part, drug buys are situations where the undercover operator has a cover person who is tasked with looking out for the operator's safety. The cover person is the operator's ticket back to the outside world. They take the notes and the drugs and whatever other evidence from the operator, if the operator has bought drugs that they need to get rid of right away. The cover person looks after all the mundane details that you don't see glorified on a television rendition of a drug bust. But these are the realities that make for successful policing.

For me, a lot of it was simple common sense. Certainly, the course was eye-opening and gave me some great ideas. But I wasn't starting out from scratch. I was already street-wise, having honed my people skills by walking an inner-city beat for eight-and-a-half years.

Except here's what management doesn't tell its black RCMP members — you will inevitably be the one that is asked to procure drugs. You won't be the one setting up the operations or making the calls. You will be the one with your ass on the line, both in terms of having harm done to you and doing harm to yourself.

Black members should also know that the difference between what management asks you to do and what you wind up doing may be significant. Management might approach you and say, "Calvin, this is only a short-term operation." And it may well be.

On the other hand, often you get into an operation, and the next thing you know there are other players involved. Things get complicated; other jurisdictions need to be negotiated with and involved. Suddenly your short-term operation is a two-year operation. And when it's all over?

You can count on another two years of going back and forth to the courthouse. For the next two years, your career is on hold, and you'll only be given menial jobs while the case is in progress. And remember, you were just the low-level operator buying the drugs in the first place. You weren't involved in the planning. You weren't in those meetings with the other departments or whatever. So don't expect the glory or the promotion when it's all wrapped up. And don't count on moving towards a stable investigator's job, or any other type of more responsible police work. You're just the nigger that buys the drugs. Hell, its natural. It's in your blood.

Period.

Another pitfall for black operators is that undercover operations often involve wiretaps. Sometimes the suspects under surveillance are using a different language. For example, some suspects may speak patois. Say you're a black cop from the West Indies, and you understand the patois dialect they're speaking. If you do, then you're headed straight for the wiretap room. Suddenly there you are, listening to three or four audio tapes a day, transcribing, translating and giving evidence in court. Again, this can go on for years at a time. Again, you're not the one running the investigation, delegating duties. You've been profiled, based on being black. Your existing skill set — your understanding of patois and your ability to transcribe — defines who you are as an officer. You have been boxed into a "culturally appropriate" role. And there you shall remain.

Don't misunderstand me. I did it, because that's what any young cop does. When you're new to the RCMP, you don't just say, "No thanks, I think drug work will be a dead end for my career."

Do that and you run the risk of being sidelined and

getting passed over for your entire career. Like the rest of the young cops, eager to please, I jumped at the perception of opportunity. The difference with me was, being black, my skin colour predetermined the limitations and scope of what would be asked of me.

What you also need to know is that undercover operators often go through a great deal of personal trauma. I've watched operators live the high life of fast living and easy booze every night. It's fun while it lasts. But once these operators had participated in a few drug busts, after a few years, they were hooked on the lifestyle. They couldn't come back to doing everyday street policing. Too many times, while undercover, these operators bent or broke the law and began to consider themselves above it all. They figured they were untouchable. The problem was, coming back down and getting back into a uniform or a police car after playing the high-rolling gangster was sometimes impossible. Their lives often ended in violence and tragedy.

On the flip side, I've seen some operators who went down so low — having gone deep undercover on the streets — they couldn't come back up to normal. Living on the streets for so long, they had problems re-establishing professional levels of hygiene and couldn't return to the world of time-lines and daily work expectations. They also didn't always come to happy ends in their personal lives.

I've also heard of operations where operators have become so friendly with the bad guys that they've refused to testify in court against them. They live the criminal lifestyle for so long that they fall in love with it, and they come to think they'd be ratting out the dealers when it comes time for the trial. These guys would be out, undercover, for weeks at a time. And they would be almost totally isolated from their pre-existing circle of friends and acquaintances. I guess in some ways, it's only natural that they'd cross professional lines with the very criminals they were supposed to be gathering evidence against.

Later in my career, I worked on an undercover operation in Edmonton where my feelings nearly got the better of me. My cover was to play a street person, down and out on his luck. I befriended people in desperate life circumstances. And make no mistake, they were involved in break and enters, theft, burglary and the like. But I honestly felt terrible deceiving them by buying their stolen goods. These folks were just doing what they could to survive. And here I was, busting them and making their lives worse. I'd lie to them, pretend to be one of them, then arrest them. It felt like all I was really doing was adding one more stressor to these people's lives and giving one more reason for people not to trust police officers.

What also remains unsaid is that the RCMP's regulations and policies — the measures meant to safeguard officers — while they might look nice on paper, aren't always adhered to in real life. During my time, RCMP policy required undercover operators to check in regularly with a psychologist or psychiatrist. But in all of my undercover career, I never once saw a psychologist or a psychiatrist, and I don't know of anybody who did in any of the departments where I worked. Members' personal concerns, along with their mental and physical health, were not monitored as closely as they should have been, if at all.

The RCMP's indifference to the mental and emotional well-being of its members — and not only in its undercover units — resulted in inefficiencies on the job including lost work time due to sick leave, along with far more serious issues such as addictions, substance abuse, criminality, inter-member abuse and suicides.

Whether it's because of what RCMP officers see and experience on the job, or how they've been indoctrinated and broken down, or the culture of alcohol abuse or the easy access to guns, I don't know. What I do know is I've watched members suffer, and I've watched the force, as an institution, fail its officers. And it costs lives.

The culture is so dysfunctional that when an RCMP member requires sick leave due to stress or PTSD, it's treated like a joke or a sign of weakness. They're referred to as being "off duty mad." You can imagine what taking on a stigma like that does to an already fragile mental state. You can also imagine how many officers suffer in silence, afraid of being categorized as "crazy" or "mad."

I never bought into the dominant undercover culture of isolation, self-abuse and overwork. This culture, which to a degree permeates the entire RCMP institution, but is most obvious in undercover work, demands that you relinquish your humanity for the sake of the mission.

Imagine you're undercover doing an investigation. You're out in the clubs all night, every night, then sleeping in until noon. You eat your breakfast in the mid-afternoon, then you may have a briefing with your cover person. This is your only brief connection to the outside world. Other than that person, you are totally isolated from your "normal." You're out of your usual routine and completely removed from the world you knew and the people in it, including your family and friends.

This usually goes on for three-week stretches, interspersed with quick trips home if possible. Believe me, this is tough. It plays absolute havoc with your mind. You've got this make-believe life where everything is played out in extremes. Then you've got your real life. Stability and routine can easily start to pale and appear boring in comparison.

To do this type of work, you have to be self-disciplined. But you also need to be completely detached from your emotions. Maybe the callouses and scars that years ago replaced my own emotions played to my advantage in this case. Who knows?

What I do know is that without an institutional priority placed on the psychological and mental wellness of its officers, RCMP members self-medicate with drugs or alcohol. All this is to say, if there's any way that your career — and your life — is going to take a dump as a cop, it's doing undercover drugs. Remember this the next time the call from management comes.

Years later, when I myself became an instructor at Depot in Regina, when black recruits would come through, I'd tell them, "This is what you should know about doing undercover drug work."

I would never tell them to outright refuse drug-related policing. But I wanted the black recruits under my charge to know that the request was more likely than not coming, and that it wouldn't be half as exciting and cool a job as they might initially think. Of course, at the time, wide-eyed and fresh, they'd have no idea what I was talking about. Down the road, though, I'd see them at a conference, or in uniform, a little more tired and a little more street-savvy. They'd tell me that I'd been exactly right, and that they now knew first-hand what I meant about undercover drug work.

So there I was, two years in with the RCMP. I'd done some successful drug work and had my undercover operator's course. I applied and was accepted by the drug division of the St. John's detachment. In St. John's, the alcohol flowed like water. It was a social, carefree, relatively happy city, and is still recognized and promoted, from a Newfoundland tourism standpoint, as a "party town" to go get drunk in. Like Halifax, it is also a port city, with all the international traffic that entails.

Most of the drug work we did in St. John's took place outside the city itself and was largely related to large-scale imports. Newfoundland has, for generations, been a smuggler's paradise. With a vast coastline and many, many harbours, the island is well-suited for ships running drugs in from the United States or from elsewhere. I wasn't involved in patrolling the coast looking for ships; I was more focused on the investigative side of things.

It was interesting work, but my main problem with working in St. John's was that I was a fairly well-known entity. Despite now being in a small city, I was still "the black Mountie," and I was regularly recognized on the streets. I had zero anonymity — one of the key ingredients of undercover operations. When I entered a bar, I'd hear the whispers, "See that guy there? He's a Mountie. If he's around, then something's up."

Whenever I showed up, the criminal element would vanish into thin air.

Due to my notoriety, there were certain aspects of undercover work that I just couldn't perform. I got relegated to wiretapping and surveillance work, out of sight, and spent many hours with my sizeable frame cramped into the back of a police van.

Although my undercover work was physically limited in St. John's, I had successfully completed the national course and was registered as an undercover operator. I had an undercover operator's number and was logged in the national database as someone who could be called on to do short- or long-term undercover operations. Several months into my time in St. John's, I got a call from the national section. I was asked to do a long-term undercover operation in Edmonton, Alberta.

I went undercover for a four-month stint. The work was out on "the drag," the neighbourhood where down-and-out people lived. Many of these folks were struggling with addictions, homelessness and mental health problems. It was a dire, desperate and sad four-square-block area of Edmonton.

I was turned loose to infiltrate — and then purchase from — the criminal element that was moving stolen goods. The neighbourhood was crawling with informants who took pay from both the RCMP and the Edmonton City Police (now called the Edmonton Police Service), depending on who was running the investigation. These informants, with their networks, introduced me to people who were known criminals, from whom I was meant to purchase stolen goods.

I followed my orders and began my undercover work. But there was a giant question mark hanging over the entire operation. Here I was, with desperate people in desperate situations selling me stolen goods, and I was constantly asking myself, are these folks supplying me with stolen goods — and committing crimes — because I've inserted myself into their lives and am now offering to buy them? Or are they stealing and selling goods because that's what they'd be doing anyway? And if they are resorting to theft just to get by, do they actually have any other life options, or is this a logical "career" choice on their part?

To me, the operation represented a clear example of the difference between "clean undercover" and "dirty undercover" operations. In a clean operation, the target is a bona fide drug dealer, or, in this case, a thief or a dealer of stolen goods. In approaching this type of target, you have a variety of options. An informant might introduce you to the target, or you might do a cold approach, or you can just hang around the neighbourhood and hope you get noticed. But in a clean operation, you're after a specific individual or a ring of individuals who have become known targets during the investigational phase of the operation.

In a dirty operation, you befriend people with potential criminal connections. You engage with these folks long enough that they begin to trust you. You know that these people generally don't deal in drugs or stolen goods, but that they probably know people who do. Once that element of trust is established, you ask them, "Hey, can you get me some drugs?" or "Hey, can you get me a stolen car?"

As a personal favour to you, a trusted friend, this person uses their connections to get you what you asked for. Then you charge them. Strictly speaking, this person has broken the law. But the problem is you've created a criminal out of a citizen. In every dirty operation you have to ask yourself — aside from bolstering a department's statistics, what's the fucking point?

In Edmonton, the ethical divide between clean and dirty operations bothered me — a lot. There was a lot of management-derived pressure on me to call people up and get them to steal something for me. It was as if there was a departmental investment of resources and time going on, and the expected returns on the investment came in the form of arrests — ethically warranted or not. Suddenly, I felt a lot like the beat officers back in Halifax who I'd watched go "hunting" for arrests in the black community just to bolster

their stats. The Edmonton operation wasn't about target-
ing known criminals dealing in stolen goods. It was about
making arrests to pad the department's stats and to enhance
the RCMP's reputation, as well as those of individual officers looking for promotions. Shortcuts were taken, and, in
my opinion, undeserving people were getting charged and
sent to jail.

My higher-ups in Edmonton also encouraged me to
falsify my notes, especially related to my use of informants.
Like I've said, undercover work is not as you see it on TV. In
real life, you have to write things down and take substantive
notes about what the offender was wearing, what they said,
and where they were, for example. You have to take charge
of the exhibits and get your notes down as soon as possible
after an interaction takes place.

Certain higher-ups in the operation would ask me whether
an informant was involved in a particular purchase. If I said
that they were, they would then ask me to change the details
of my notes, such as where I was when I met the informant.
Granted, changing my notes in this way would have kept the
identity of an informant better concealed. But if I falsified my
notes and I then referred to them in court, then I'd be lying
under oath. And what if the accused person knew that I was
lying under oath? Then there'd go my credibility as a witness.
I'd be perjuring myself, and I'd blow the case.

So I refused to do it.

Other officers would also tell me, "Listen, if you have to
sleep with a couple of women in the course of the operation,
go ahead and sleep with a couple of women."

There was absolutely no way I was going to do this. I was
not going to endanger my health, or be responsible for a
pregnancy or stoop to that level of emotional treachery just

for the sake of an undercover operation. From a criminal justice standpoint, undercover operators are not supposed to sleep with offenders or their associates because, again, it compromises their credibility as witnesses. It's comparable to using drugs with the targets of an investigation. But being placed in these ethically and morally reprehensible positions is just one of the aspects of undercover work that the public doesn't see.

I was pretty much on my own, out on the streets. There was one other undercover operator in the area, but we couldn't be seen together. He was lucky to be from the Edmonton detachment, so he got to go home at the end of the day. There was one handler, who was supposed to check in with me, but I guess he was happier hanging out in the safe house because I never once got a visit. I didn't have anyone from the real world to unwind with. On top of that, I couldn't go to a club or get involved with anybody outside of the operation in any meaningful manner. I never knew whether someone I had befriended in the "normal world" might come walking through the door with my main target. For four months, I was almost exclusively on my own.

Unfortunately, a couple of people moved into the neigh-bourhood who recognized me from my boxing career. Because of all the media hype that was associated with my boxing, they put two and two together and tagged me as a former cop from Halifax. Until that point I was doing well in my undercover role, but being recognized burned the whole operation.

So . . . it was back to Newfoundland.

The problem was, back in St. John's, in my absence, the sergeant in charge of my subdivision had reassigned me back to my old detachment in Holyrood. To me it felt like a shady move to make. Here I was, busting my ass for the force, living one step up from homelessness, undercover for the past four months, letting my emotional health suffer, and no one bothered to tell me that I was going to be reassigned to an undetermined detachment somewhere in Newfoundland.

I was unnerved. I didn't know what was going on, career-wise. I did know, however, that I couldn't go back to Holyrood. I thought about packing it in and leaving the RCMP. Without much in the way of options, I met with the commanding officer in St. John's, and I gave him a pitch I had been thinking on.

I said, "Look, I want to stay in drug work. Let me head west to Toronto. I'm sick of being the only black Mountie. Transfer me out to a multicultural environment where I can actually blend in. You know and I know that I've got what it takes to work in undercover, if only people didn't spot me on every operation."

I'd been warned by other members, in different ways, that black officers in the RCMP ought to stay the hell out of Toronto Drugs. But although it was never my intention, I had become a journeyman cop, and I was sick of sticking out on the island, like the lone blueberry in a bottle of milk. Despite the dire warnings of rampant racism in Toronto, I went for it. My transfer to Toronto was put through. Finally, I thought, I would be in a city of millions. On top of that, some of my family, who I'd never spent time with, actually lived in Toronto. I figured I would finally have my anonymity.

CHAPTER 7

SURVIVING TORONTO DRUG SECTION

Before I arrived, I had heard all the stories of Toronto Drugs chewing up black cops and spitting them out. The place was famous nationwide for its racism. I figured I was tough enough — I was a heavyweight fighter who knew how to take a punch and stick with the plan. My birth father was a sixth-generation black Canadian who was shot in the gut in the Second World War and kept fighting. No way I was going to be chased off my chosen career by a bunch of white supremacists in uniform.

Going in, I had a solid track record. My paperwork was all in order. My write-ups and assessments — the trail that follows you around your career in the RCMP — from my years in St. John's and Holyrood were all positive. I was in fighting shape, I was capable and for the time being, I still had some degree of faith in the RCMP as a whole. In the end though, none of it counted for shit; not any of my positive write-ups or my shiny smile.

See, when you make a lateral transfer from one province to another, nobody knows you, and nobody cares how good you were before you got there. If you haven't got the connections, then it's "so sorry, man," you're back on the bottom rung making your reputation all over again.

On my first day in Toronto, I went to get my building pass. I produced all my documents — my RCMP identification, my letter of transfer. I laid out everything neatly across the front desk of the office building. The civilian employee at the desk, without even glancing at my paperwork, nonchalantly said, "Well, nobody knows you here, so I can't let you in. Go find somebody who knows you and come back with them."

This was not a good omen of things to come.

When I finally made my way in the building, I found out that Toronto Drugs was, to put it bluntly, a total cesspit. There was unprofessional stuff going on all over the place. From what I could tell, there were zero ethics and no moral code of behaviour. I like to think that I didn't head to Toronto Drugs without having seen some things in my life, but I was honestly shocked. It was like Dr. Joe Dietrich's worst nightmare had come to life.

There was rampant alcohol abuse. There were barely functional alcoholics in positions of authority. Reportedly, members would drive unmarked squad cars to bars and get so drunk, they'd forget where they'd parked. They'd have to get help from other members to find the car the next day. It's said that on one occasion, a member was so drunk that he crashed his unmarked car on his way to the bar. He just left it and stumbled back to the station to get another car.

There was also an alleged incident when a member was caught on security camera in the exhibit room sniffing seized cocaine. A sergeant was known to be having an affair with his counterpart from the U.S. Drug Enforcement Agency (DEA).

It was as though RCMP headquarters had turned a blind eye, and Toronto Drugs had been left to fend for itself, free to abuse its authority and live by its own twisted code of conduct. This zoo was my new workspace, so I settled in as best I could.

As with any alcoholic family, every member is complicit. I found my space — I had to. It was either that or face complete ostracism and isolation. As usual, I played the role of the enabler. I was the stone sober cop, driving a car full of drunken Drugs squad officers across Southern Ontario, in search of booze, debauchery and fast nightlife. I'd drive them over the border to Buffalo, New York, so they could get wasted at the DEA Christmas party. They'd get completely hammered, and then I'd load them all back in the car and drive them home at sunrise. I'm not proud of it but that was the dysfunctional family that I belonged to.

There would be times when we'd go out for lunch. It would start with a drink, and the next thing you knew, everybody would be getting drunk, and we'd call off the rest of the day. On more than one occasion I had to figure out who was supposed to meet with whom that afternoon and call ahead and cancel all the meetings that were going to be missed due to drunkenness. Over cups of coffee and split lips, members often bragged about the fights they had started the night before.

A few months in, I was working on a drug investigation in which we had wired up a hotel room for purchases and exchanges. The wiretap was being worked out of an adjoining room. At one point, I was left to work the wiretap for twenty-four hours straight without a shift change or even a change of clothes. I don't know if I was simply forgotten, or if it was some kind of sick test; nobody came to relieve me.

During that particular investigation, when the wired hotel room wasn't in use, a DEA agent and an RCMP officer would be having a romantic liaison in the room. I guess they just wanted a bed and four walls so badly that they didn't care that the place was wired for sound. And recording! I remember the one officer warning me, as though the whole thing were some kind of joke and *I* was the pervert, "Now Calvin, don't be listening in on the wiretap when the operation is not ongoing!"

Not all of it played out like some sick joke. It might sound disgusting — and it was — but these were also real people with real addictions, in need of real help that they seldom got. More than one member wound up committing suicide or spending serious time in jail. In other instances, this false sense of power and entitlement didn't confine itself to the workplace. And the results were sometimes horrific. Patrick Kelly, who was later convicted of first-degree murder for throwing his wife off of the balcony of their apartment, had worked in Toronto Drugs.

At the time of my transfer to Toronto Drugs, there were four units. I was assigned to the cannabis unit, which was kind of a catch-all unit. I don't say this lightly, but it was akin to working at a Ku Klux Klan affiliate. Some members in my section threw the word "nigger" around like it was wedding confetti. A number of RCMP members in the section were either passively or actively racist; it seemed to be part of the culture. Not one person stood up against it, and I suffered because of it.

One of my first interactions with a Drugs squad member — a man I hadn't known more than a few days — took place after work hours in the office. He approached and waved me over.

"Cal, come on over here."

It was just the two of us in the office. I went over. He had a mugshot of a black man in his hand, a side and front view of somebody I guess they'd just arrested.

He said, "D'you see this?"

I looked. Somebody had written the words "Monkey Man" across the mugshot.

He asked me, "What'd you think of this?"

I didn't respond. I just stared at him hard.

"Cal, the guy's just a nigger. He's a just nigger, man."

At this point in my career, I was too smart and savvy to be race-baited. I told him, "You know what? I think that this guy was on his way to the First Baptist Church for prayers, and some white guy here just fucked him up for no good reason. That's what I think happened here."

Then I walked away, leaving behind a foolish — potentially drunk — co-worker with a stunned look on his face. It's a lesson I learned from boxing, you never let your opponent know that you're tired or injured. For every nigger comment, nigger this or nigger that, I'd come back with a comment of my own about the general stupidity of white people. It was like sparring with an office full of opponents, and in some twisted way, it became part of the camaraderie.

I never let myself get physical in these situations. While it might have felt nice, you knock one guy out at work and poof, that's the end of your career. At the end of the day, though, I'd annihilate the punching bag at the detachment gym. Some of my co-workers would also be at the gym, working up a sweat on the treadmill, and they'd see what I could do to a bag. For what it was worth, I was still the toughest man in the building, so they never got serious with me to my face.

When I first arrived, Kenny Gibson was the only other black member in Drugs. At one point, Kenny was approved to take French language training, to which, as a long-standing member, he was entirely entitled. After he left though, I overheard another officer comment, "What d'you have to be to get anything around here, a nigger?"

For a while, that left just me in the lion's den.

A few months later, Rob Aiken, another black member, transferred in. Rob was a judo master, so nobody really picked on him either. Through it all though, if I wasn't aware of the degree to which Rob and I were actually suffering, I was becoming aware that other black members were not prepared for, nor were they tolerant of, this type of racist behaviour. Some black members simply couldn't take the racial harassment in Toronto Drugs and had their postings cut short.

Lynell Nolan and Roger Crowley, for example, two upstanding black RCMP members, had been in Toronto Drugs prior to me. I know personally that they couldn't stand the toxic environment and transferred out. Instead of RCMP headquarters doing anything about reining in the brutal racist behaviour in the office, it seemed to be simply accepted that Toronto Drugs was the place that white supremacists went to play. It was just engrained in the culture. It wasn't a place where black officers were expected to survive, let alone thrive to our full potential.

Nothing was done. We just took the abuse or moved on. I endured it for a period, but what was going on in the Drug Section was a clear violation of the ethical and moral policy of the RCMP. None of us black members should ever have had to put up with this type of bullshit in the first place.

Over my years working in drugs, I found that the deepest

pockets of racist behaviour were in the drug sections of the larger Canadian cities like Edmonton, Toronto and Vancouver. I draw the parallel to the days of slavery, where the most problematic slaves — the ones who didn't "know their place" — would be sent the furthest South, to the most brutal plantations. The attitude in these drug sections seemed to be, "Bring the big niggers here, and we'll break 'em in for you."

On the positive side, working in Toronto was the first time that I'd been anonymous in my policing career. Anonymity meant being able to leave the office and not be pegged as "the black Mountie" until my next shift. I clocked in, did my job and clocked the fuck out. Nobody was going to track me down and demand answers from me when I was off duty trying to get a bite to eat, or take in a movie, or have a date or whatever. Nobody was going to hold a grudge and try to get even with me or come at me simply because I wore a police uniform. When the day was over, I became just another one of the faceless millions. At work, despite the rampant alcoholism and racist behaviour, I still tried in vain to earn the respect of my peers and supervisors. I still operated under the code that the merits of your work, no matter who you are, should determine whether you are promoted to higher levels of decision-making in an organization. Organizations with a deeply racist culture, however, destroy this mirage for you. They will never share the institutional power with a person of colour. The culture simply will not allow it. In fact, they will fight you for it.

The RCMP policy at the time was that institutional promotions were supposed to be based on job performance, as demonstrated in your assessments and scores. The system was supposed to be blind to race, gender, sexuality and religion. The problem was that the assessments and scores — the key to promotions and access within the organization — were in the hands of racist supervisors. If you don't look like one of them, then your accomplishments stood to be minimized and your opportunities restricted. Through the white supremacist lens, when you're black and working hard, your hard work is interpreted as a threat. The harder you work, the more of a threat you become. And, in turn, the harder the system pushes back against you.

In the Toronto office, beyond the usual racial jabs, there were other, more sinister, examples of racist behaviour. There were the sneak attacks — the anonymous posters and notes and letters whose origins I could never trace.

For example, one day I came in to work after a lecture that I'd given to an outside organization. The lecture had been well received, and I'd been congratulated for my efforts. Waiting for me in my note basket on my desk was a scrawled note saying, "Fuck off, Nigger." About a week later, I arrived at work to find a "Nigger Application for Employment" form on my desk. The form contained a disgusting list of the worst racial stereotypes.

On another occasion, our detachment was relocated to another building. We were set up in cubicles, and there was a poster taped to the outside of one of the cubicles. It was a caricature of a black man with an afro hairstyle and big, accentuated lips and nose. The caricature was naked, running in bare feet. It was a firing range target, and scrawled across the top of the poster were the words, "Official Runnin' Nigger Target."

This poster was visible to anyone entering the Toronto Drugs office. Because we regularly worked with other departments on undercover operations, our office was a high-traffic area. The poster would have been seen by RCMP supervisors as well supervisors from other departments and members of other police agencies, such as Toronto Police Service and the United States DEA.

This sign was permanently displayed at Calvin's workplace within the Toronto Drug Section.

And just like back in the day in the Halifax police writing room, nobody batted an eye at this poster or said a word about it. Nobody did anything about it. Nobody even thought to take the poster down.

Let me ask you this, if you went to work every day, and that poster was on the outside of one of your co-worker's cubicles, what would you think about the values endorsed in that office?

Is it safe to say that this was a bastion of white supremacy?

If this poster that promoted murdering black people for sport was acceptable, what else was acceptable?

Remember, this is the RCMP I'm talking about. The venerable, vaunted Canadian institution.

If you use racial slurs when you speak to my face, I can gauge whether you're a hate-filled racist or just trying out the sound of a new word as it leaves your lips. When I hear your words and read your body language, I can adjust my reaction accordingly. I can perform my own verbal judo on you. But when you sneak around like a coward, leaving notes and putting up posters, you may as well be burning crosses with your hoods on. You're a racist and a coward, hiding in anonymity.

I've always refused to be intimidated, but I was shaken. I dismissed the notes and posters as cowardly bullshit. What concerned me more deeply, however, was whether these same people — who were obviously my co-workers — would be there for me when I needed them in an undercover operation.

Would they protect me as a brother officer and keep my safety at the forefront of their minds? Or did they really actually think I was a nigger who should just "fuck off," or worse?

This conundrum weighed on my mind whenever I did an undercover job. These were real-time situations that required teamwork and trust, that carried with them real risks and danger. Here I was, a hard-working cop who was trying to get drugs off the street so that your kids didn't get hooked. But given the types of blatant harassment I was experiencing out in the open in my workplace with "Fuck off, Nigger" and "Nigger Application" notes left in my work basket, and an "Official Runnin' Nigger Target" poster on the cubicle wall, I honestly worried about whether I'd be shot in the back by one of my co-workers, let alone by one of the armed drug dealers we were supposed to be trying to bust.

Doing the actual undercover work itself was another area where the racist behaviour was on display. For the most part I was relegated to local, undercover drug work. Major international undercover drug duties were never, ever, assigned to us black members. The major international investigations went to members with connections in the ranks — in other words, to white officers. The international investigations were the high-profile, elite operations where commendations and promotions were earned. Other members went to France, Mexico and the United States. I went down to Bloor and Spadina.

As for my direct supervisor, I can only describe him as a workplace sociopath. He would load me up with work. And I was a bachelor and still hoping to prove myself, so I'd come back at night, after my shift, to finish my assignments. I'd be there on weekends doing all the extras.

In the local operations, my supervisor would go out of his way to make sure that I didn't get to participate as an equal. I did the wire room. I did pre-raid surveillance. I did the transcriptions. But when it came time to do something like a court-authorized surreptitious entry — something that involved teamwork — he'd say, "Nope. Leave Calvin outside. He's not coming in on this one."

Exclusion is a form of racial harassment.

One time, he and I were doing surveillance of a target in a parking lot. He was in his car, and I was in mine, parked next to him. Unrelated to the target, there was a group of black men playing dominoes outside at a nearby residence. They were loud and having a good time, and we could hear them shouting over the game.

The sergeant leaned over to me and said, "Straight out of the trees, eh?"

The comment speaks for itself.

More troubling, I'd overheard several civilian co-workers working in the wiretap room talking with him, and he would specifically ask them, "So . . . how's Calvin doing?"

They'd reply, "Good, good. Why? What's going on?"

He was obviously trying to dig up dirt on me. He was on a personal mission to smear my work credibility. He wanted to restrict my opportunities and limit my accomplishments. By this point, I'd started keeping my own notes and making photocopies of the racist notes and posters that littered my desk and office space. The whole unit, my supervisor included, must have seen these things, and I'd documented a long list of incidents in which he'd harassed me in various ways. As far as I could tell, he was trying to find a way to discredit me. Given that I was one of the few black members who just wouldn't leave, maybe it was a plantation-style challenge for him to break me down.

After a few months of taking notes on him poking around concerning my workplace comportment, a civilian colleague approached me and said that she had heard enough and was willing to go on the record about this sergeant making unnecessary inquiries about my work. With that offer in hand, I made my move. I wrote up my own report and went to the inspector in charge of the Drug Section. I showed him my photocopies.

I negotiated my own transfer to another section of Drugs. I said, "I don't want to file a complaint against this sergeant. But I do want to be moved immediately."

The inspector seemed alarmed. He was all, "Yeah, yeah. Okay, okay." He had known the whole time exactly what was going on in my section. He also must have known that I now had solid grounds for a complaint that would disgrace the unit and the RCMP, if he forced my hand. I got my transfer.

Before I left the unit, the sergeant called me into his office and said, "You know, Calvin, when you get promoted you're going to be very upset when people go behind your back and go over your head." Then he added, "They probably wouldn't have even hired you in the RCMP except that you had previous policing experience."

"Why is that, sir?" I asked, staring him down.

He had no answer for me. We just stood there, looking at each other.

He had set the rules. But if he was going to try and play me, I was not going to stand by and let my career be ruined. I wanted to tell him that if he came at me, I'd come right back at him with what I had.

I wanted to tell him, "You're an incompetent supervisor and a workplace sociopath, and I know that you've had something against me from the minute I walked in the door. But you're not going to break me. Because I can work you — and anyone like you — under the damn table."

Looking down at this sergeant, I had Malcolm X's words on the tip of my tongue, "I'm the man that you think you are. You would have to die and be born again to become the man that I am."

I left and went to work for a different unit. But trust me, the toxic cloud of racism was smeared all over Toronto Drugs.

Now, of course, on top of being black, I was a trouble-maker. I was a not-to-be-trusted note-taker. To the racist mindset, my desire for workplace equity just made me one more untrustworthy "angry black man" who wouldn't play with the team. Word travelled, and I was viewed with suspicion. There were whispers and looks, and everybody thought I was running around keeping notes.

I became numb to it all. If you asked me now, "How did it feel?" I'd have no answer for you.

Those years are lost to me emotionally. All I can really do is relay the facts. I thought of my father, taking abuse on the railroad, coming home all bottled up with shame and hurt. I never wanted to take it out on anyone, a wife or a family. So I isolated myself. I didn't drink, but I punched the bag until my hands bled through the gloves.

Throughout all of this, I was still able to complete my assignments and be heavily involved in numerous drug investigations. During these operations, I often worked with members from Toronto Police Service as well as RCMP members from other units. The majority of these men and women were there to do their jobs professionally and were competent at what they did. They weren't sniffing for promotions or practising racist behaviours. This must not be lost in my experience of the Toronto Drug Section. But it was clear that it wasn't an environment where I would flourish or make a life.

Having been on the job for several years, I'd become a seasoned undercover operator. Again, I was into what should have been promotional range. But the scoring system got you in front of the promotional board for interviews for available positions. In the hands of a racist sergeant, my scores were kept very low. My write-ups were great, but now I was experiencing the refinement stage of racist behaviour.

Jumping off from Neely Fuller's *The United-Independent Compensatory Code/System/Concept*, I have learned that white supremacist behaviour — not to be confused with white behaviour — is established, maintained, advanced and refined.

I've observed and experienced the 'establishment phase' from the times of my first memories, up to and continuing through the present day. To me, the establishment is indicated by ongoing racial conflict which has intensified and subsided — ebbed and flowed — throughout my lifetime.

The 'maintenance stage' is perpetrated in ways that allow for manipulative, racist structures to be set up, towards giving maximum advantage to dominance and control of black people.

The 'advancement stage' of this process means that white racist behaviour will always follow us as black people.

In the refinement stage, the tactics and strategies utilized by white supremacists are more covert. Rather than call you a nigger, they simply will look for more subtle ways to advance their racist agenda. As it stood, I was trapped. Pigeonholed.

In the RCMP, at that time, we had no union. Instead, we had a division representation system. Members of a division would elect a representative, who was supposed to advocate for them and stand up for the membership's rights. The division rep was someone who members were theoretically able to approach with work-related issues, ideally someone who had the qualities of a listening ear and a helping hand. If there was anyone to whom I could turn — outside of my immediate workplace environment — this might have been the one.

A guy who was running for our divisional rep came down to our office to give a speech. All of us in the Drug Section went there to hear him out. After he left, we were all sitting around, asking each other about him — what he was like, who knew what about him as a person. One of my colleagues piped, "Well, his career was blossoming. Until he married that black girl."

I sat there. See, it wasn't a matter of me not fitting in. It wasn't a matter of not being "one of the guys." It was a matter of me being black.

Plain and simple.

CHAPTER 8
KEEPING WORLD LEADERS SAFE

In 1987 I was thirty-eight years old, trapped in the racist cesspool of Toronto Drugs. I'd been a cop for almost twenty years now, and life as a police officer wasn't working out the way I'd thought it would. Toronto as a city offered me bright lights, anonymity and plenty of opportunities and diversions. But I was no longer operating under any illusion of being included as an equal in the drug unit. Far from it. I was more concerned with catching an errant bullet from one of my co-workers. My work in the Drug Section was stellar. But career-wise, it was a total waste of time. Toronto Drugs was a dead end — figuratively and potentially literally — for a black cop.

Try as I might, I couldn't escape being typecast as the cool black guy who'd be naturally skilled at procuring drugs from other black guys. That was the breadth and scope of my use in Toronto. And sure, it was exciting work. But it wasn't going anywhere. And I kept getting assigned to these undercover operations where I was supposed to score drugs from black dealers from the West Indies. Other than the fact that we were all black, we had nothing in common. These guys were from a variety of Caribbean islands, and I was from Nova Scotia. Despite our fairly similar appearance, there was a massive cultural difference between us — different foods, different religion as well as a very real linguistic barrier. I could not speak, or really even understand, their patois. We'd take one look at each other, and they'd know that I was in the wrong place. And nothing would come of it.

The gig was getting old fast, and I put in an application to be transferred out. I kept my ears open for transfers and promotions; at that point I was willing to go just about anywhere to get out of Toronto Drugs. But it was like I had to peel their fingers off my wrist to get them to let me go. The section was drowning in its own toxicity and dysfunctionality, and I had to fight not to get dragged down with it.

That's the way it works. When you're in, they think you're in to stay, and you're not releasable. Management informed me that because I had applied to leave the Drug Section, I was no longer eligible to take any drug-related courses that might expand my professional skills. Not like they would have let me anyway. At the same time, I was told that because I was in drugs, I was ineligible for any non-drugs courses.

It was a career catch-22, and I interpreted it as a feeble attempt to get me to roll over and say, "Okay, okay. I'll stay in drugs."

In retrospect, with all professional avenues closing down around me, my golden ticket out fell into my lap.

While working undercover drugs, from time to time I was getting seconded by the Toronto Protective Policing section to do site security duty, which was called "VIP policing." The Protective Policing section in Toronto was comprised of eight full-time members. With such a small staff, whenever an internationally protected person visited our city, or when a large-scale event was held in town, the full-time members would second more suits on the ground. To meet their needs, Protective Policing would second additional officers from other sections in Toronto. It was a temporary gig, but it was a breath of fresh air.

Internationally protected people could be the cook at an embassy, the leader of a country, or anything in between. The level of protection that Protective Policing provided to their "VIP" depended on the threat designation they were assigned by the Canadian government. The visit or event might be a simple meet-and-greet, a low-key lunch date or a full-blown motorcade with a red-carpet stop and a press scrum included. It could be an official visit or the covert visit of a VIP on private business. While it wasn't a necessary prerequisite to being seconded, regular RCMP members could sign up to take a VIP course to learn the various duties, which included bodyguarding, site security and site surveys, as well as driving motorcades and related duties.

Generally, if you had the VIP course under your belt and you were seconded by the Protective Policing section, you would be assigned to an active posting in the operation. This might include driving in a motorcade or bodyguarding the protected person. If you didn't have the VIP course, you were usually assigned a static post. This generally meant that you stood a post at a site — guarding a door, for example.

Having seen VIP operations in action and having been seconded to work a few operations as a static officer, I became interested in this specialty. I requested to sign up for the VIP course to expand my range of duties beyond static posts. If I could enroll in — and complete — the VIP course, I knew that I could foreseeably transfer out of Drugs and into Toronto's Protective Policing section. Once in the Protective Policing section, the door would open to more varied protective policing duties such as working economic summits and visits from heads of state, royalty, spiritual leaders and other dignitaries. With all other options shuttered, this became my exit strategy.

I applied for an upcoming VIP course scheduled to be held in Ottawa. My application went to my immediate supervisor, then up the management chain of command for consideration. The response came back to me that since I was not in the Protective Policing section, I could not enroll in the course. I knew that this was a bullshit excuse, and it also confirmed my suspicions that steps were being actively taken to limit my career opportunities in the RCMP.

This was now a common thread throughout my decade-plus as a black RCMP member. Some nonsensical reason would be created to explain why I wasn't allowed to take a course or perform a duty. I'd do a little investigating, and I'd find out that the same reasons being given to me actually didn't apply to someone else — someone who wasn't black. Then, when I spoke up or fought for the exact same opportunities that my co-workers were getting without having to undertake the same struggle, I'd be labelled a troublemaker or get accused of being overly ambitious.

In this case, through my own research, I came to know that the rest of the officers enrolled in the upcoming VIP course were not actually working in the Protective Policing section. In fact, through the water-cooler chatter around the office, I found out that two officers from Toronto Drugs

Calvin and the RCMP security detail for Princess Alexandra of Great Britain in Toronto in 1986.

had been approved to take the VIP course. It was totally counterintuitive; officers needed to complete the course as their first step towards getting transferred into VIP policing, not the other way around.

I went to my divisional rep and asked why two members from my section of Toronto Drugs had been approved to attend the upcoming VIP course in Ottawa. They weren't in Protective Policing — they worked in the same office as me. A few days later, I was informed by my supervisor that my name had miraculously appeared on the list of those approved to take the VIP course. So off to Ottawa I went.

The course entailed two weeks of presentations and demos. We learned bodyguarding, shooting and driving, as well as how to conduct pre-visit site surveys and security placement. At the end of the two weeks, the class performed a hands-on, full-blown mock scenario of a protected person's visit using a written plan that we'd prepared as a class. Our simulated visit involved the co-ordination of motorcades, the placement of active and static bodyguards, undertaking site security and site surveys, and developing a fully functional operational plan. Our goal, as in any real operation, was to successfully protect our VIP from accidental or intentional harm. Each aspect of the operation had a co-ordinator who worked with the team. VIP work, as I came to learn, was a team effort.

Once again, the difference between Hollywood's hyper-individualized rendition of protective policing and real-life protection was staggering. In VIP policing, our team's goal was to minimize the possibility of having any actual encounters with negative elements wishing to harm our VIP. The aim was to never embarrass the VIP by having confrontations with the public or anyone else, especially in front of cameras. No surprises. No emergencies. No individual heroics for the press. No leaping in front of shooters with an epic soundtrack in the background. Everything prepped and accounted for.

We definitely did learn some of the Hollywood skills. But, as a VIP operator, if you ever find yourself in that kind of situation — diving into crowds, tackling protesters to the ground, chasing a gunman, whatever — it means you've been out-planned by somebody. When that type of shit goes down, it means it has been an unsuccessful VIP operation. On the day of an actual operation, the only thing an event co-ordinator should have to do is advance their team through each site of the pre-planned route. As opposed to the Hollywood version, the aim of Protective Policing is to make every operation run like a very boring, uneventful movie.

I successfully completed the VIP course and subsequently brought my documentation to the RCMP inspector who liaised with Toronto Protective Policing. He leafed through my papers, looked up at me and said, "Just because you've completed the course doesn't mean you're going to get into Protective Policing."

"Aha. Now this is why I was initially refused the course," I thought to myself.

It wasn't some mystery; this inspector was just one more racist in a position of power who didn't want a black man working on his unit.

I went back to working Drugs for a few months. But having completed the VIP course, I was seconded into an increasing number of VIP operations. Taking on active positions, I was getting into bodyguarding, working the motorcades and generally getting a taste of the various aspects of Protective Policing. It got to the point that I was checking for my photograph in the local newspapers because at the same time as I was guarding protected people, I was still doing my undercover drug work. I was working with some high-profile VIPs in public situations, and having my photo shared around Toronto's Caribbean community wouldn't be good for my covert operations.

Pulling double duty between Drugs and VIP lasted for about two months. Then, by a stroke of good fortune, there was a staffing change; Toronto Protective Policing had a new inspector in charge. I'd made it explicitly known that I was looking for a transfer, and with this particular roadblock cleared, a civilian member in Staffing determined that there was no reason why I couldn't transfer to VIP. I got the hell out of Drugs.

Leaving Toronto Drugs lifted a huge weight off my shoulders that I didn't realize I was carrying. Suddenly, in VIP, I was in a place that I loved, doing a job that I loved. I could dive into my work, and I was good at it. For the time being, the yoke of racism was off my neck.

In VIP, depending on the level and type of visit or event that you were preparing for, the logistics of seconding members from other sections could be enormous. An economic summit or a first ministers' conference might each need fifty members or more to take care of the various duties associated with the event. We at Protective Policing were the department in charge of the visit, but we'd co-ordinate with other departments, both inside and outside of the RCMP. Toronto Police Service, for example, were in charge of the city while the Ontario Provincial Police (OPP) were in charge of the province's highways.

I personally had a long list of VIP assignments for which I was responsible. Depending on the visit, I'd be involved in various stages of the planning process. If I was doing support, I might be driving a VIP vehicle, or doing a site survey or running and timing motorcade routes prior to a VIP's arrival.

Calvin with election campaign security detail in Toronto in 1987.

Eventually, I began taking charge of operations and co-ordinating entire visits. This involved working with Toronto Police Service, the OPP and airport security. If the prime minister was visiting, for example, I'd also liaise with his office. I'd delegate duties to various policing departments. I'd ensure that the visit plans and itinerary were up to date and shared with the contact people who needed them.

At the planning stage, I'd designate motorcade routes, co-ordinate bodyguard teams, decide on site security and conduct site surveys. Depending on the time of the visit, I might have to set up site security in the middle of the night and put police vehicles in place. During a visit, I sat at a desk with two phones — one to my ear listening to a conversation, while I was leaving messages on the other. If I was the visit co-ordinator, members, regardless of rank, reported to me. I was also accountable for any problems or incidents.

Sometimes there were complications and glitches to deal with. But in my experience, I can trace the majority of these wrinkles back to the actions of VIPs themselves rather than to the professionals tasked with ensuring their safety.

For example, during an election, the heads of the official political parties each have VIP security provided to them on the taxpayer's dime. During election season, party leaders frequently have political fundraisers — get-togethers that cost one thousand dollars a plate for dinner.

At these events, do you think they want a police officer on security detail sitting beside them? No. Not at all. The politicians want to be rubbing elbows with campaign donors. At their fundraisers, they would often put up a fuss and try to keep me and my team from doing our jobs. But if I'm doing security, then I'm doing security, and I'm calling the shots. If not, then I may as well go home. I can't

place my protective detail at the back of a room filled with
five hundred people and expect them to protect their VIP if
there's an unexpected commotion. It simply can't be done.

If you think about it, some of the most infamous political
assassinations and assassination attempts happened when
the VIP ignored the advice of the protective team. George
Wallace's team in Alabama told him not to go into the
crowd. Wallace went into the crowd and got shot five times.
Ronald Reagan's team told him to keep the press lines back.
He didn't, and Hinckley infiltrated the press line and shot
him. J.F.K.'s team in Dallas told him to leave the top up on
the car. He told them to put it down . . .

On top of that, sometimes you'd get a VIP asking you to
do things that were beyond what we as security were there
to actually do. For example, we have VIPs telling us to "go
get tickets for the play," or "take the laundry to the cleaners"
or "go walk the dog."

I'd calmly but firmly remind the VIP that the protective
team was providing a service, and that the service was security, not running errands. Simply put, I can't do security and
hold an umbrella over your head when it's raining. You have
to hold your own umbrella. If I'm holding the umbrella,
then I might be watching you get shot.

I personally got a real thrill out of planning VIP security. I was contributing. I was keeping people safe. I was
solving problems on the fly. I was making snap decisions.
And I was very good at it. I negotiated with other police
services, security officers from other countries, and sometimes the Prime Minister's Office. I worked closely with the
United States Secret Service when their former and current
presidents came to Canada. I was directing other RCMP
members. My preparations were meticulous, and nobody

Calvin working as part of the RCMP VIP security detail for ex-President Jimmy Carter in Toronto in 1988.

got hurt on my watch. And that includes both intentional and accidental harm.

From a political perspective, I didn't allow my own convictions or beliefs to interfere with my professional approach. I was certainly aware that I was being charged with providing security and safety to individuals whose track records — in terms of human rights abuses — were less than stellar. Perhaps nowhere was this more evident than when our unit provided security to the South African consulate in Toronto. This was in the late eighties, when there was extensive global protest against the South African apartheid regime. There I was, a black man, putting my own body on the line to safeguard representatives of that oppressive regime.

I rationalized this paradox in the following manner: An assassination of a political representative from a foreign country on Canadian soil was totally illegal and would not have any positive outcomes whatsoever, political or otherwise. If I turned the other way while the South African ambassador to Canada got killed, it wouldn't actually end apartheid. No matter who was under my watch — dictator, king or democratically elected leader — I treated them the same.

In a professional environment, I flourished at my work. After a couple of years, I volunteered to lecture on the VIP course circuit — the same course I was initially told I wasn't allowed to take. The first course for which I lectured was in London, Ontario, on the topic of site security. Over the years, I lectured on all aspects of the VIP course, including bodyguarding, site security, site surveys, site surveys specific to hospitals, site placement, motorcading and some aspects of self-defence. I lectured on a volunteer basis while continuing to work VIP in Toronto.

During this time, I was also taking night courses at Humber College for a certificate in international terrorism. The way the political world was developing its priorities, I could see that terrorism was going to be an up-and-coming issue in the policing sphere. At Humber College, we were taught about the various aspects of national, international and transnational terrorism, and how to prepare ourselves as law enforcement professionals.

I also became part of the Members Assistance Referral Program. The program was initiated to provide assistance to RCMP members who were having problems for which they needed outside help. At the Referral Program, we listened to them and made suggestions for referrals to professionals or specialists. For example, if someone had a drinking problem, or was suicidal or had domestic problems, we would refer them to the appropriate resources. I had always been interested in family pathology, childhood trauma and family-of-origin issues. I had first become a police officer to help people — all people, including my co-workers. This was one way that I could help my colleagues in distress.

I did all of this while I was still a constable; I had never been promoted in over ten years with the RCMP. But as a VIP security co-ordinator, I was directing and educating members well above my rank, including inspectors and superintendents.

In 1988, the World Economic Summit was held in Toronto. Leaders from around the world came to town, and it was a massive VIP security operation. We had to plan driving routes, sites and motorcades months in advance. Because the VIP section had visits to plan on a regular basis, aside from the Economic Summit, a major task force was put together just to plan for the Summit.

Calvin bodyguarding Prime Minister Brian Mulroney and Mrs. Mulroney in Toronto in 1988.

When the Summit took place, members from the VIP section were given major duties. Things were not up to scratch, mostly because of the larger-than-normal number of units associated with the event. But we took what we had, and we made it work. I was in charge of the bodyguard team for the then–Prime Minister Brian Mulroney. There were a few hiccups due to planning errors, but I fixed them all. RCMP Inspector Moffatt was Mulroney's travel officer at the time. Moffatt was impressed with my resourcefulness and quick thinking. The good impression I made on him would put us together again in the future.

Later in 1988, in Moncton, New Brunswick, the prime minister's wife, Mila Mulroney, was struck with a picket sign at a protest. Someone had gotten too close to her. Mulroney wasn't injured, but within protective policing circles the incident was seen as a team failure. And as a result, the RCMP decided to form the Prime Minister's Protection Detail (PMPD). Rather than having protection duties delegated to the various local protective sections wherever the prime minister might be, the PMPD was to be exclusively responsible for protecting the prime minister and his family. The PMPD would be the prime minister's full-time, travelling security detail.

With the new team being assembled, there was also a need for RCMP travel officers, usually with the rank of inspector, to do advance reconnaissance trips to wherever it was that the prime minister was going. The travel officers performed pre-visit site surveys, and then would brief the rest of the PMPD on their return about the upcoming trip. These travel officers would also check in with the local police to ensure that their security was up to standard and would provide these bureaus and departments with the logistics of the upcoming visit, along with the person-power they were expected to provide and roles they were to play.

At this point, I was lecturing at the national VIP training courses. I was a seasoned trainer and presenter in all aspects of the training. I applied for the PMPD, along with a number of other members from Toronto VIP. To me, it was a natural fit and the culmination of my years of work in protective policing. Three other members from Toronto were accepted and transferred without a hitch. For whatever reason, I was accepted on paper, but Toronto Protective Policing tried to derail my transfer.

I got a written notice saying that my transfer had been okayed. Ottawa had approved it. But Toronto did not support my transfer. No reason was given. I did some checking through contacts that I'd established at Staffing in Toronto. I found out that VIP in Toronto was trying to keep me in there. The justification that they were floating was that they were concerned about losing all their local experts to PMPD.

There may have been some truth to this. But nobody in Protective Policing came to me to tell me as much. Nobody said, "Look Calvin, we can't afford to lose you right now. How about you hold off for six months?" There was no communication whatsoever. Instead, it was basically just a "lost" transfer slip. Three other officers from my unit — officers I'd had a hand in training — got fast-tracked to PMPD while I was expected to wait.

If I hadn't spoken up, I imagine that I would've sat in Toronto with a transfer slip in my hand, wondering why my co-workers were moving on while I stayed behind. To add insult to injury, the three other officers in Toronto Protective Policing heading to PMPD had significantly less experience than I did. I was one of the best officers in the department. I was training people above my rank, all across the country.

Once again, there I was, wasting my time, sanity and energy, fighting for something I was qualified for while the door was held open for those less qualified. And once again, the lines of open and honest communication between me and the RCMP bureaucratic machine had shut down. I made it known to Staffing that I was prepared to take legal action about having been treated unfairly. And lo and behold, once I spoke up, I was transferred to the PMPD, just as the team in Ottawa had requested.

When I left, I was presented with a Certificate of Appreciation from the United States Secret Service. I had worked closely with their office in Buffalo, New York. I was also presented with a plaque from the Toronto Police Service VIP section and a pin from the OPP VIP section. Even if the RCMP itself hadn't let me know, it was meaningful to me that I'd made such a positive impression on my co-workers in other departments.

United States Secret Service
Certificate of Appreciation

Presented to

Constable Cal Lawrence
VIP Section
Royal Canadian Mounted Police
Toronto, Ontario, Canada

in grateful recognition for superior contributions
to the law enforcement responsibilities of the
United States Secret Service

Issued in the City of Washington, D.C.

Given under my hand and Seal in the year
1989

Director, United States Secret Service

Certificate of Appreciation from US Secret Service, Toronto, ON, 1989.

CHAPTER 9
OTTAWA BOUND

In 1989, I drove from Toronto to Ottawa to find a place to live. I scoped out the downtown area and rented myself an apartment. I was a single journeyman cop. My job had become my life. My tastes in accommodation were simple, and I didn't need more than the bare basics. In a couple of days, I had my needs, such as they were, sorted out.

My initial task with the PMPD was to merge all the ad hoc VIP duties associated with the prime minister from what had been, until that point, the purview of various municipal police services in the national capital region. I turned these into a set of full-time duties for our newly formed team. The Ottawa Protective Policing section, which had been, until that point, the lead unit on the prime minister's protection, would still provide security whenever protected persons came to town. Ottawa Police was responsible for everyone except for the prime minister and his family. That was now our job.

Calvin working for Prime Minister Jean Chrétien's security detail in Budapest, Hungary, in 1991.

Calvin in the White House Press Room in Washington, DC, in 1992 as part of the Prime Minister's Protection Detail.

When I arrived at the PMPD, they had a two-person training unit tasked with bringing the new members up to speed. Those of us who'd been selected for the PMPD from across the country all had pre-existing qualifications, so the training unit's role was to enhance and review the protective training we already had and bring us under one skill-set umbrella. The training unit was also meant to keep our skills sharp for doing site security, bodyguarding, driving and more. We were divided into four teams of between ten and fifteen members each. Our schedule was four days on, four days off, with training such as target practice on top of that.

We constables now attached to the PMPD in Ottawa were expected to do bodyguarding, motorcading and site security. We were basically meant to fill the active VIP roles. But back in Toronto, as a constable, I'd done all that and much more. I'd been involved in co-ordinating every aspect of VIP visits and events. In addition, I'd lectured and taught all the VIP skills, which included travel officer duties, across the country.

In Ottawa, travel officers — each with the rank of inspector — were tasked with organizing all the advance work related to the prime minister's travel schedule. The travel officers were at the top of the pecking order, and we constables were their eyes and ears on the ground. We would supply the travel officers with security information, and if need be, they'd relay it back to the prime minister.

On a normal day, when the prime minister was in town, we'd pick him up at his residence and drive him to his office on Parliament Hill. The constables would be assigned to one of several different positions in the motorcade, riding in either the limousine or in one of the two security vehicles accompanying the prime minister's limo. The rest of the day, we would do site security or personally bodyguard the prime minister. We would have a schedule of his comings and goings as well as his wife's and children's schedules. The whole family got security, and we might be assigned to any one of the family members, depending on what was happening that particular day. At the end of the day, the prime minister's team would drive him back to his residence. If there were any evening events scheduled, we'd provide security for those too.

For the general back-and-forth routes within Ottawa, the PMPD team usually didn't develop a specialized operational plan for the day. If the prime minister was going to a function in Ottawa that was out of the regular schedule, then the team might put together a route, do a site placement in advance and draft an operational plan for that particular event. The bodyguard team might walk the route to the hotel, and do a site assessment on it prior to the event.

On pre-event walk-throughs, we'd be looking for anything unusual. Anytime there's an organized attack, the perpetrators will have done their own reconnaissance prior to the attack. We'd constantly be looking for evidence of a plan, a guy digging a hole on the side of the road for six months, a woman pushing a stroller that didn't look right, whatever. Our job was to keep on top of anything suspicious, including things that might cause accidental harm, such as trailing wires on the floor or low-hanging equipment.

Although there was extensive travel with the prime minister, it wasn't something I really looked forward to. Whenever I was on assignment with Toronto VIP, the team stayed in the same hotel as the protected person. I'd also done years doing undercover drug work, sometimes going weeks without a comfortable bed under me. During those years, I became well-acquainted with the lifestyle of subpar food, roommates and uncomfortable beds. Still, I saw the world and travelled with the PMPD to Singapore, Russia, the United States, Italy, Germany, France, England and Iceland, to name a few. But once we got to our destination, there was very little site-seeing involved, and the job itself was always pretty much the same. We did our security checks and lived to ensure the prime minister's safety.

In 1992, one of the two PMPD trainers was transferred out of the section, creating a job opening in the training unit. I applied, and because of my extensive experience teaching national VIP courses, along with all of the planning and co-ordinating work that I'd done with Toronto VIP, I was given the position. As a constable in the field, I had had no problem doing any of the associated duties with the

PMPD. But unlike my fellow constables, I also had years of on-the-ground experience in managing and troubleshooting all aspects of protective services. While I was still utilized in the field when the need arose, my main duties shifted to arranging and providing ongoing and remedial training for established and incoming members of the PMPD.

I literally began to train my supervisors. I would take inspectors, who'd joined the PMPD to become travel officers, through the necessary VIP courses. The courses were run by the Central Training section in Ottawa. Sergeant Ed MacDonald was responsible for the VIP course design and administration, and he always struck me as a professional. Under MacDonald's guidance, candidates for VIP were monitored very stringently, and course instructors were held to a high standard of performance and delivery. I enjoyed the strict organization protocols he demanded

Calvin with Corporal Al Cyr, the director of the US Secret Service and an agent in 1993.

Calvin working as part of the Prime Minister's Protection Detail in London, England, in 1992.

and looked forward to every day I had the good fortune of working with him.

Some officers tried to pull rank when they were over-whelmed with the training and blame us, the instructors. For most of them, it had been a while since they'd been put through a rigorous training program. But MacDonald would have none of it. He documented the good work of the instructors, and I have his commendations in my file along with my annual assessments. In my mind, the RCMP would have to go a long way to find another supervisor as competent as him.

As for training the newly arrived travel officers, we'd give them presentations on bodyguarding, site security, site surveys, motorcade driving and formations and how to put it all together into a functional operational plan. They also had to pass a firearms course. Then we'd run them through mock visits, and I would mentor and critique them. I prepared written reports on the state of their progress. Then we'd come back to Ottawa, where they'd become my bosses as travel officers.

In many cases, because they were new to the job, I would continue to mentor and monitor travel officers as they settled into their active duties. On one occasion I was made an acting travel officer and accompanied other fresh inspectors in performing their duties. Coincidentally, on that occasion, I'd trained both of the travel officers I was accompanying.

As an in-service trainer, I had the opportunity to go to a protective briefing given by the United States Secret Service in Beltsville, Maryland. This briefing was a run-down of all aspects of the protective detail that the Secret Service provided for their president. Upon our return, we submitted a report on how we might extract aspects of the Secret Service's methods and put them towards improving the protective capabilities of the PMPD.

It was interesting to compare the American approach towards safeguarding the president against how the PMPD operated. For their part, the Secret Service generally shut down streets and kept the public far away from the president whenever possible. In comparison, at events and in general, in Canada the prime minister was fairly available and accessible to the public.

This cultural quirk added certain complexities to our job. We had to be hypervigilant in our approach to protection, as the public's access to the prime minister was not usually screened during the events. The prime minister might be visiting a farmers' market, or attending a parade, or doing any number of events where the point was for him to mingle with the crowd. In the PMPD we had to ascertain, throughout the course of the event itself, who might be a threat to the prime minister, all the while doing our best to protect him from instances of accidental harm as well. Rather than sticking to firmly established protocols, as did the United States Secret Service, the intensity and scope of the security surrounding the prime minister was largely driven by his own attitudes and behaviours, as well as those of the entourage surrounding him on that particular day.

Although the PMPD demanded the utmost in professionalism, there was a constant culture clash that seriously detracted from the capabilities of the unit. Specifically, there were deep divisions between the French- and English-speaking members on the team. Anyone who has ever been to Ottawa, or, more particularly, anyone who has ever worked a government job in Ottawa, is familiar with the underlying tensions that exist between Francophones and Anglophones, especially as they relate to promotions and jockeying for advantages in the workplace. Unfortunately, the PMPD was unable to escape this issue, and at times it played havoc with our ability to protect the prime minister.

You might ask why everybody in the PMPD wasn't bilingual. Canada is, after all, an officially bilingual country, and services must be provided in both languages. Realistically, however, there are only a few pockets — across a massive country — where bilingualism is actually required to properly do the job. In these pockets, French is dominantly spoken. Ottawa, with a large Franco-Ontarian population and its proximity to Quebec, is a bilingual area. But the majority of the country, from a territorial perspective, speaks English and is not actually bilingual.

Insofar as these geographic realities applied to the PMPD,

we were constantly on the move, following the prime minister's itinerary across the country and around the world. On our travels, when we were in another RCMP division's jurisdiction, we'd inevitably be in need of seconded members from that division to assist in site and route security, depending on the venue that the prime minister was to visit. This meant that our team had to work with the language requirements of the jurisdiction in which we found ourselves.

In parts of Western Canada, the majority of RCMP members speak English only. If, on the other hand, we were in Quebec or in some international locations, the members you'd be seconding might speak French only. In both situations, bilingualism was a nonfactor. Instructions would be delivered in English — or French — only. Delivering instructions in a language the locals couldn't understand would put the safety of the prime minister and his entourage at risk. But within the PMPD, there was this constant push-and-pull between members who only spoke English and members who only spoke French.

The workplace tension was real. Some members were hardcore French speakers and wanted to speak only French while doing their duties. This was dangerous because you'd have people on the ground who really couldn't understand what was going on. It put us all, including the PMPD team, in danger. It was strange because as a team, we were supposed to be doing everything possible to minimize risks to the life of the prime minister and his family, and ourselves.

Sometimes there was bantering. Some French members would say to me, "Oh, you speak English. You're with the English."

Then I'd have English-speaking officers say, "You're one of us."

And I'd say, "No. I'm not. I'm not Anglophone. I'm 'Black-o-phone.' There were no Brothers on the Plains of Abraham. This is your issue."

To be clear, I was always well respected by the members who spoke French as well as the RCMP members who worked VIP in Quebec. Even in Quebec, at the time, VIP courses were only taught in English, and as an instructor I'd played a major role in the French members' professional development. And no matter what their mother tongue was, I always treated course participants with honesty and respect. I was a tough instructor, but your language, skin colour, gender or religion had nothing to do with how I evaluated you or turned you into a capable VIP officer.

The bottom line was that we'd been put together to do an important job where we were putting our lives on the line. If the bullets started to fly, then language and race issues went out the window. Everything except securing the situation went out the window.

In comparison with some of the shitholes I'd worked in, I wouldn't say that the PMPD was a racist workplace. I do, however, remember one poster that got tacked to the PMPD office wall that portrayed certain members as dogs available for adoption. In this poster, the other black member on the PMPD and I were caricatured as dogs named "Blackie" and "Spook." Again, it was an anonymous poster that nobody took responsibility for — and nobody objected to — that set the tone of the office. In 1992, nobody in the PMPD thought it was racist that I was being called a dog named Blackie.

But what to do?

My job was to guard the prime minister's life with my own. I just looked at it and said, "This is definitely a poor attempt at humour." I took it off the wall and added it to my ever-growing file folder of racist posters.

In the PMPD's two-person training unit, my counterpart — the other trainer — was a corporal. I'd been with the RCMP now for fifteen years and had not received a promotion; I was still a constable. At first, the difference in our rank wasn't an issue, and shortly after taking on the position, I became an acting corporal, the next rank up. I hadn't been officially promoted to corporal, but with my expertise, experience and work ethic, I figured it was just a matter of time.

About then, a call came from the RCMP in Nova Scotia requesting that I transfer back home. This wasn't the first time that the RCMP had attempted to bring me back to the Maritimes. In 1992, the long-simmering disputes between the black community and the RCMP had once again reached a boiling point. Management in Nova Scotia mentioned that if I returned, I could get promoted and maybe become a commissioned officer. They wanted me to drop everything and return because apparently the Nova Scotia division still couldn't work with the local black communities. This wasn't anything new. Perhaps they should have sent me back to Nova Scotia when I was first hired. Now, as a seasoned VIP trainer with my career finally on track and set for advancement, I was not about to be their black face in the right place. I refused.

If I had thought that I'd be given the opportunity to reshape policy and introduce meaningful interactions — and change — to the relationship between the RCMP and the African Nova Scotian community as a whole, I'd have gone in a heartbeat. Decades ago, this had been my dream. But I was too seasoned a police officer to jump through the hoops placed in front of me just to be racially showcased in an ultimately meaningless position. So I stayed put in Ottawa.

With the PMPD, I assumed that my skill set and experience would keep me in the trainer's position and would give me the inside track on any promotional developments. At that point, I'd been performing my duties as an acting corporal for almost two years. I had also become an expert in protective policing and was consulted by colleagues and forces from across the country.

Finally, in late 1992, Staffing determined that the discrepancy in rank between the trainers was an issue that needed to be addressed. They couldn't have a constable — me — and a corporal — my co-worker — doing the same job.

As I saw it, in this case Staffing had three options open to them. First, they could lateral in another corporal by making the position available to officers who were already corporals. As I was still just a constable, this option would keep me out of consideration for the position. Second, they could downgrade the second trainer's position to constable. Or, third, they could advertise the trainer's position as a promotion to corporal. I was already doing the job, teaching VIP skills on the national level, and my assessments and scores were consistently above average. After fifteen years with the Mounties, I figured I would finally get my promotion.

Initially, Staffing determined that they would lateral in another corporal, and that the position would have a bilingual requirement. This meant I'd be squeezed out of my job. When I approached management, the reason they gave me for the bilingual requirement was that my counterpart in the training unit, who spoke French, might go on vacation. I informed them that was true. Between 1990 and 1992, the man had definitely gone on vacation. But no one during the last two years had ever had a problem with me being the sole trainer during his vacation. I saw the language card being invoked because there was now a promotion at stake. And after so many years of dealing with racism within the force, I did entertain the possibility that they specifically didn't want me to have the job.

Past behaviour is the best predictor of future behaviour.

Wayne Martel, then the superintendent in charge of the PMPD, regarded me well and supported me for the position — and a promotion. On my behalf, he wrote a memo to the managers in Staffing saying, "The corporal you're going to lateral in is not as capable as the constable who is here. And the constable who is here should be promoted."

He gave me a copy of the memo and said, "This is the best I can do for you."

And that was it.

While the position was up in the air, Martel moved on. A new superintendent, Marcel Groulx, moved in. Initially, I didn't have a lot of contact with Groulx. I was still in the training unit, and I was consistently doing good work. I was, however, curious about his thoughts on the trainer position and the progress towards filling the second position. At my request, Groulx met with me on August 11, 1993. To my face, he said, "I've heard a lot of good things about you." He assured me that he supported the promotional process in place for the position that I had been occupying for over two years.

This certainly sounded good to me. In a promotion scenario, I figured that my assessments, scores and experience would speak for themselves.

The next day Groulx had the Staffing action held in abeyance. This means that he attempted to suspend the staffing change for the trainer position. He'd iced the entire process. Groulx never told me he'd done this and kept me in the dark about this important development. I only found this out months later, by doing my own Access to Information request for the Staffing file.

This tactic was introduced to me by a member back in Toronto Drug Section, who told me I could get my medical file, my personnel file and my service file — and any other files that the RCMP were holding in respect to my career. We didn't have the internet at that time, but I was quick to realize how Access to Information requests could be applied to anything that was written or said about me that was documented. As the months went by and the bureaucratic web began to tighten around me, I used the requests to my advantage on numerous occasions.

The months went by, and I continued to work in the PMPD training unit, in some kind of employment limbo. I heard nothing regarding my position — whether I'd be promoted, transferred, rendered redundant. Nothing. On October 10, 1993, I wrote a memo to Staffing inquiring into the status of the training unit position, specifically whether or not a promotional board was going to be held. I also provided a copy of this memo to Superintendent Groulx.

Later in 1993, for reasons I have never been able to understand, Groulx lowered my scores on my annual assessment. As I've explained, with the promotional process at the time, it was these scores that got members before the promotional board. If Staffing did decide to undertake a promotional process rather than a lateral promotion, these now-lowered scores would ensure that I never got before the board. To me, it looked like Groulx had a beef with me and was doing his best to squeeze me out of my job.

In the eight years I'd been with the unit, I had become one of the best VIP/PMPD members in Canada. I was an expert trainer. I was dedicated, knowledgeable and well

respected across the country. And finally, I was on the cusp
of my first promotion.

Now it felt like it was all for nothing. Just another dream
deferred.

When I received my 1993 assessments, I read Groulx's
criticisms of me. In writing, he critiqued me for doing
police community relations work in high schools across the
Ottawa area. RCMP policy clearly encouraged its officers
to undertake community involvement, such as speaking to
students in high schools. Community relations work was
done on a purely voluntary basis, outside of my duties with
the PMPD. On my official assessment, he wrote that, due
to my community work, I may have lost track of my duties.

I was shocked.

Once again, I perceived the refinement stage of racist
behaviour kicking in. In light of the lowered scores and poor
assessments, I informed Groulx that I would be appealing
my assessments. I let him know that I was aware that he'd
lowered my scores, and that there was no valid professional
reason for him having done so. If *my* assessment scores were
low, and I was one of two people in charge of training the
entire nation's VIP staff, then what the hell did that then say
about everyone else I'd trained? Did Groulx have something
to say about the quality of content of the national training
program itself? The quality of travel officers in charge of the
prime minister's life? Or was it actually just some personal
problem he had with me?

I appealed my assessment through the proper channels.
RCMP management's reaction was swift.

Behind my back, the officer in charge of training
and development surreptitiously went to Sergeant Ed
MacDonald, who was in charge of running the national

VIP courses, and attempted to get him to blacklist me from teaching the VIP courses. MacDonald, always in my corner, informed me of the measures that were being taken against me. He also refused to remove me from the course instruction roster. He needed good instructors and was not about to be swayed by shady bureaucratic machinations against me. Appealing my assessment was my right under RCMP policy, and now covert attempts were being made to punish me for having done so.

I contacted a lawyer. His response, when I presented him with all the documentation I had gathered on my file, was, "Calvin, are they ever fucking you around!"

With MacDonald vouching for my professionalism and refusing to buckle to the backstabbing manoeuvres, and with my legal intentions now being made known to the RCMP, Groulx tossed me a bone, he made me an acting travel officer. He sent me to Arizona with two other travel officers, both inspectors, both of whom I'd trained. Our mission was to protect retired Governor General Ray Hnatyshyn. I suspected that Groulx, and whoever was working with him behind the scenes, wanted me out of Ottawa temporarily — and out of direct contact with my lawyer — while management figured out their next move against me.

Regardless of the drama brewing up around me, I did the work that had to be done as a travel officer. I did the advances for Mr. Hnatyshyn's visit and did a few things that greatly streamlined his motorcade and enhanced the safety of the entire trip. One of the travel officers gave me a 10-04, a commendation that is added to your annual assessment. But I wasn't appeased by getting a tan in the Arizona sun. The trip just proved that I was competent, and that I could hold my own as an inspector, let alone as a corporal.

I wanted my fair shot at the trainer's job, and a few weeks as an acting travel officer in a low-risk operation didn't wipe that from my priority list.

On December 8, 1993, I spoke with a certain Sergeant in Staffing. He told me he was finally going to answer the memo I'd written back in October — over two months earlier — concerning the status of the trainer's position. In our conversation, he stated that a staffing action had never been requested for my current position.

When I later obtained Groulx's notes from August 12, through a subsequent Access to Information request, it showed that indeed there was a staffing action that had been requested. Without a doubt, it showed that Groulx had had the staffing action held in abeyance. In fact, the notes I obtained show that it was *the same Sergeant* who had met with Groulx in August. Now there were two names known to me — the Sergeant and Groulx — who were actively engaged against me. Had either of them been forthcoming, honest and informative with me as to the status of the trainer's position I currently held — and intended to apply for permanently — I would never have contacted a lawyer. Instead, they had machinated behind my back for months as though this were just a game to them, and my career was entirely expendable.

As I saw it, now with Staffing and my direct supervisor working against me, I had no recourse — or reason to trust — in the existing system. I filed a complaint of racial discrimination with the Canadian Human Rights Commission (CHRC).

Having now been through the process, I believe the CHRC operates using flawed logic. When the CHRC receives a complaint, they should first speak with the complainant — which they did. Second, however, they should investigate the complaint. As a police investigator, to me, this means doing interviews and gathering evidence from the people the complainant has named in the complaint. But the CHRC doesn't actually do this.

In my case, the CHRC never even interviewed Groulx, my current supervisor. They didn't interview Bourgeois in Staffing. They didn't interview Martel, my former supervisor, or my co-workers at the PMPD — or anyone else, for that matter. Instead, as was standard practice in racial discrimination cases, my complaint was redirected from the CHRC to the Diversity Management section of the RCMP.

Under this protocol, the Diversity Management section then solicits responses from all the involved parties. Diversity Management returned its package of responses — internally gathered, pre-filtered and sanitized — to the CHRC's office. Aside from interviewing me, the CHRC played no role in gathering data. And so, the brunt of the investigation was internal to the RCMP. The people I accused had time to prepare their responses. They had time to deploy linguistic camouflage to justify their actions. I'm not necessarily saying they lied to staff at Diversity Management. I'm just saying the process as it exists is seriously weakened by not having CHRC investigators conduct their own independent investigation and speak directly with all the individuals involved.

It is my opinion, having subsequently worked in the Diversity Management section, that the bureaucratic response is more along the lines of "Shit guys. How do we get out of this one?" than "Okay. Let's find out the truth and tell it, no matter who it helps or who it hurts."

In my opinion, the CHRC also doesn't understand — and therefore seldom looks at — the refinement stage of racist behaviour. It either doesn't know how to, or it cannot rationalize it when it sees it. There I was, my position cut, my performance scores lowered for no reason, formally criticized for doing more than my job description, and my memos to Staffing going unanswered. I had done nothing wrong, but my entire career was being derailed by unwarranted criticism and behaviour incongruent with RCMP policy as it related to its employees. But unless somebody called me a nigger to my face, according to the CHRC, nothing being done to me was racially motivated.

Ultimately, the CHRC dismissed my complaint. I was dejected, to say the least.

A few days later, at the suggestion of an acquaintance, I called a prominent Ottawa-based lawyer. I presented my case to him, and he decided that I had enough to start a civil suit against the RCMP. He informed the RCMP of our intentions and put them on notice.

At the same time, I paid a visit to an advocacy organization called the National Capital Alliance on Race Relations. This organization was run by Dr. Shiv Chopra, a scientist who had had his own case, over his whistle-blowing on the safety of meat products in Canada, come before the CHRC. Dr. Chopra took an interest in my case and began to act in an advocacy role on my behalf.

Weeks later, while instructing a VIP course in Winnipeg, I was called by Dr. Chopra and asked whether I wanted to go to the press. I was still in employment limbo, and still livid about the way I'd been treated. I said, "Fuck it. Yes. Go for it."

Newspaper headlines in Ottawa the next day read, "PM's bodyguard claims racial discrimination."

Then the shit really hit the fan. It was "Heavyweight cop not allowed to compete at Olympics" all over again. Except that now I had seventeen years of abuse under my belt and was better prepared to fight my opponents.

I contacted the Visible Minority Advisory Committee, which operates within the Diversity Management section. The advisory committee is made up of individuals of different ethnic backgrounds who advise the RCMP Commissioner on multicultural issues. They advise on, but they are forbidden to get involved with, individual issues. I went to them anyway and told them what was going on. The committee was unable and unwilling to violate their mandate — all except for one person. Caroline Thomas, a fellow Nova Scotian, agreed to help me.

After my appeal to the advisory committee, Thomas spoke with me personally and said, "I'm going to address this. But I'm going to address it privately with the RCMP commissioner." I don't know what transpired during their conversation. Afterwards, however, things started to change.

Subsequently, I was approached by RCMP Assistant Commissioner Curt Allen, the director of personnel in Ottawa. He told me that he wanted to know how I'd been wronged. He told me that he wanted it on plain paper, specifically not to be written on RCMP stationary. He also told me that he didn't want it sitting on "some secretary's desk," and that he wanted it hand-delivered by me to him. This type of request speaks for itself. In my opinion, Allen's approach was intended to legally protect individuals — Groulx and whomever else — as well as the RCMP as an institution, from any further evidence of wrongdoing.

I typed up the facts of what had happened, keeping a copy for myself. On a Saturday morning in June 1995, I went to Allen's house and gave him the written description of my case. Standing at his front door, Allen looked at me and said, "This doesn't mean you're going to be promoted."

"I know," I replied.

I thought, "You just circumvented the whole system. Do you think that if I'm not promoted, I'm not going to tell someone what just happened here?"

Ultimately, I never went in front of the promotions board. In August of 1995, however, I was appointed to the rank of corporal by then-Commissioner Murray. The appointment was backdated to February 29, 1992, when I'd first started as an acting corporal with the PMPD's training unit.

Back in the PMPD office, however, the vultures were still circling my career.

One of my final assignments with the PMPD was the 1995 G7 Summit in Halifax. I was to assist with the training of "H" Division members from Nova Scotia in all aspects of VIP duties. Inspector Moffatt had observed and recognized my talents when I'd been in charge of the bodyguard team for Prime Minister Mulroney at the 1988 G7 Summit in Toronto. He now requested that I lead the bodyguard team for U.S. President Clinton and supervise the bodyguard team for Hillary Clinton and the Clinton entourage. The Clintons were arguably the top VIPs in Halifax. Moffatt knew I could think on my feet, take decisive action when necessary and troubleshoot problems quickly. I didn't know it then, but the G7 in Halifax, my hometown, was the end of the line for me in the PMPD.

Word circulated in the RCMP that I couldn't stay with the Prime Minister's Protection Detail. I'd caused too much of a ruckus. I'd exposed Superintendent Groulx and publicly accused him, in the press, of screwing me over for a well-deserved promotion. On top of that, I'd accused the force of racism. The cult of the glorious red serge would not stand for being maligned like this. In my mind, I could just see the long line of people with their knives out, ready to carve me up.

On the other hand, consider my actual motivations. I'd caused this so-called "ruckus" because my direct superiors had attempted to sideline my career. All I had ever wanted was the chance to get a promotion to the same rank as the guy working beside me, doing the very same job I was, and to simply stay where I was doing what I loved. For years, I'd put the life of the prime minister and his family — not to mention that of every visiting dignitary who'd come through Toronto — before my own, and look at how I was treated.

Sure, I could have applied for anything, anywhere within the RCMP, and maybe I would've gotten an opportunity to be promoted and treated fairly. I could have gone back to Nova Scotia and acted like a good Uncle Tom, promoted as the new black sheriff in town, smiling and nodding while nothing actually changed in the RCMP's policy towards African Nova Scotians. But why should I have had to submit to this song and dance to get a promotion? Couldn't I just be black *and* be judged based upon my actual abilities? I was among the best in the PMPD, and the promotion was right there for the taking. Could I do the job? Hell, yes. I'd been doing it in an acting position for two years.

A number of RCMP members would later say that I was treated this way because I was English. I would shoot back, "How do you know? With all the covert actions that were undertaken against me and never even explained to me by the members who committed them, then tell me how you know that?"

Some RCMP members will always be racists. And the people who practice white supremacist behaviour are insecure. I was a competent, dedicated, ambitious black member. That scares the hell out of people who display racist behaviour.

They say to themselves, "Shit. I have to do anything I can to stop this black man. He is just as good or better than me."

The Black Panthers had packed up and gone home, their memory gone dusty with age. The turbulent sixties were long past. But the adage remained the same; to those in power who practice white supremacist behaviour, equality looks a lot like oppression. Power is not relinquished without a fight, and those who control the institutions will not give it up peacefully.

So don't tell me why I've been treated the way I've been treated. Not when I have a file folder filled with a Runnin' Nigger Target poster and Application for a Nigger notes.

In 1995, I was promoted, but I had no more job. At the same time, my father passed away. I also had to take care of my ailing mother back in Halifax. I was a corporal that the RCMP needed to find something to do with. In my heart, I knew that they were going to make me suffer for having exposed their wrongdoing.

The question was, could I pay?

CHAPTER 10
STRUGGLE FOR SURVIVAL

I had embarrassed the RCMP. Publicly.

It didn't matter that I was right, or that I had received my promotion in the end. I was informally disowned by the alcoholic dysfunctional family. I wasn't even the enabler anymore. What I had done was unforgivable. I was a pariah. An outcast.

Have you ever been ostracized, yet still been physically present?

Set adrift in a sea of averted eyes?

Trust me, it's not a good feeling.

It was made obvious to me that I had to leave the PMPD. It didn't matter that I didn't want to go. The goal had never been to get my promotion and then be forced out of the unit where my expertise lay. I had worked ten long years in protective policing. I had woken up each day willing and ready to put my life on the line. Or take a life, if need be. It broke my heart that I couldn't stay in the area of policing where I was one of the foremost international experts. I wanted to stay in the PMPD either in the training unit or as a member. All I had ever wanted was equity.

The dispute, however, was not over yet, and the bureaucracy needed to get in its parting shot at me. If I didn't go along with what they now wanted, which was to move me out of the PMPD, the bureaucratic machine would have ground me down to dust. I'd have been fighting management and Staffing every day. I would've seen Groulx every day, after having publicly embarrassed him. I would have been sidelined from meaningful duties for the rest of my career.

In dispute situations like mine, it's as if the organization is running a relay race while I'm forced to run a marathon. Every day, they bring in a fresh angle, a fresh runner whose job is to figure how to get me shuffled out to pasture as quietly and quickly as possible, and make it look as though they're doing me a favour in the process.

The organization has the power and the money. I had no money, and I was on my own. I had to accept some of the choices they made for me and reconcile myself to those choices. They made me offers to move me out of the PMPD. What they offered didn't feel fair or just, and it didn't give me any satisfaction. It all just got to a point where I thought, "Okay. I can live with this. What I can't live with is staying with the PMPD any longer."

I knew that I would not — and could not — give up my integrity.

I really don't know how it all went down in the end. Maybe some managers in Staffing dreamed up the scenario that they could make my promotion and subsequent expulsion from the PMPD look like it had some kind of a positive racial connotation attached to it. I don't know what these

Calvin attending George Washington Slave Memorial Service at Mt. Vernon in Washington, DC, in 1996.

people talked about when they sat down together at board-room tables. I don't know how the plans get incubated and hatched. But ultimately, I was offered a lateral transfer and a position in the Diversity Management section — the same section that had dealt with my human rights complaint.

Maybe management figured that this was the best that could be made of my prickly situation. As a salve to a black man's anger — and the RCMP's bruised reputation — I could be racially showcased by putting my minority status to work for them. Once again, like a broken record, I would be the black face in the right place. Going to Diversity Management and working for — and with — the people who'd fought on behalf of the RCMP against me was salt in a too-fresh wound.

When I got to Diversity Management, I was accepted and treated fairly by the civilian member, Dieter Schachhuber, who was in charge of the section. Professionally, I had dealt with Schachhuber before. In the office, we had some long conversations about race, the RCMP and life in general. He understood me on an intellectual level, but like with most white people, there remained a distance between us. I got the read from him that he was a caring man who had taken some heat over the course of his career for trying to do the right thing.

Working alongside Schachhuber was rewarding, but the rest of the building had their knives out for me. It was like being stranded on a hostile island, surrounded by danger on all sides. I knew that I was despised by a number of people, especially officers, for the public stink I'd raised against the vaunted RCMP. I'd embarrassed Groulx — one of their own — and in the pervasive cult mentality, I'd embarrassed them all. In the command-and-control environment of the RCMP, a slight against the organization was taken personally by a lot of members. At Diversity Management, I'd walk into a room and the collective body language would go cold.

In my understanding, it all went back to the mass indoctrination at Depot; the red serge was infallible and never to be challenged. For all the RCMP members who worshipped at the foot of the commissioner's photo, the prevailing feeling around Ottawa was that in embarrassing the RCMP, I'd embarrassed them by extension.

At the office, if I parked in the wrong place, members from other sections at Headquarters would file complaints against me. My co-workers were waiting for me to fuck up and ready and willing to call it in when I got something wrong. Wherever I walked, there were whispers and snide remarks in the hallways. And as I was to learn, the organization has a long memory and carries deep grudges.

So why did I carry on in this toxic atmosphere?

Despite the impact that this type of work environment was having upon my mental health, I had borne witness to the treatment my adopted father had suffered through while out on the railroad. I thought of my ancestors — escaped slaves. Their determination through adverse conditions gave me a deep well of strength. Back then, there was no Human Rights Commission. There was no harassment policy. My birth father fought during the Second World War alongside white men who wouldn't speak to him when he got back to Canada.

I come from people who come from people who come from very strong places. If life gets hard, then you work harder. And that's what my parents taught me. At night, as I conjured their memories, I knew I could not let these people down.

I will say this, though, I was stretched as far as I could be, emotionally, mentally, spiritually and physically.

Despite the pangs of loneliness that bore down on me

from time to time, going through what I was being put through, I still felt lucky that I didn't have children or other immediate family at this point in my life. I wouldn't even have been able to walk the dog; all my energies were devoted to steering the course of my work-related problems. I had become a focal point for raw, racist power in action.

In the course of my career, I've seen other members who've had spouses, children, car payments, mortgages and all the responsibilities that go with them. Stretched thin with commitments, I've seen those members break under the strain of racial abuse. I've seen some members harm themselves, even commit suicide. As a single black man, it was difficult. But if I'd had family or been heavily in debt? There's no way I could have carried on.

Now, as I relive these memories, stressed and sleepless, I learn that Krista Carle, a lead complainant in a sexual harassment case against the RCMP, has committed suicide. All she and the other female officers in their case wanted were meaningful careers with the nation's policing force. When Carle died, I believe that a bit of every one of us who has gone through major clinical depression, anxiety and post-traumatic stress disorder at the hands of the RCMP died as well. Too many RCMP members minimize, deny, ignore, repress or disassociate themselves from the racist or sexist behaviour on the job. I've seen it take a long time, particularly for some black members, to self-destruct under the weight of racist behaviour. I've watched many of my co-workers go downhill on the "instalment plan." Divorce, mental health problems, alcoholism, unhealthy attachments and more are all symptoms of the pain caused by unequal treatment within the RCMP.

I think of Jane Elliott, the teacher and trainer behind the

famous "blue eyes, brown eyes" experiment. As Elliott has consistently shown, when you put a bunch of white people in a room for three hours and treat them like black people, they can't stand it. They go crazy and leave.

We can't leave.

In Diversity Management, I was a "race relations advisor." Going into a job with that kind of title, I naively thought I'd be able to improve race relations within the RCMP. Eventually, as the days turned to weeks, sitting at my desk, I realized I was simply a casualty, lost in the fog of politics. I was being put out to pasture, left in some corner cubicle to go numb. It was disappointing, but not surprising.

I remember one morning, not long into my new position, receiving a phone call asking me if I played golf. There was a tournament involving some high-rolling black civilians, and the RCMP needed to field a black man of their own on the greens. I guess my new handlers were testing the waters, checking to see if I'd go quietly off into the world of golfing buddies and fake smiles for the camera.

They wanted a golfing, storefront house Negro!

I replied that I didn't golf. The unknown voice on the other end of the phone replied, "Well, maybe you should learn!"

My retort was, "*I* box. Maybe *they* should learn to box."

Nobody called back.

Basically, my job, such as it was, consisted of assisting the Visible Minority Advisory Committee that reported to the RCMP commissioner. I arranged for committee members to attend conferences. I booked their hotels and made their travel arrangements. I set up their conference rooms for their meetings and made sure they had pitchers of ice water to drink. I also researched whatever topics the committee

STRUGGLE FOR SURVIVAL 203

might be presenting to the commissioner. I took notes and wrote up reports on the meetings.

To put it bluntly, it was all a waste of fucking time. I was a seasoned field officer, with twenty years of combined policing experience, filling up carafes of water and making sure the napkins were properly folded. It didn't take long for me to realize that Diversity Management, as a section, was designed to spin the wheels of process. I could contribute to race relations, but only through the pre-structured confines of office politics. Real-time, problematic issues, such as endemic racism and sexism within the force, were not actually meant to be addressed or resolved. The imperative was to keep discussion surrounding the issues going so that it would look like progress was being made, when in fact nothing was happening at all. It was like being tied to a treadmill, never going anywhere. My duties and contributions were controlled to the point that everything I did was meant to reflect a circular process.

The sad thing was that, in the two years I spent there, there was never any attempt made to create a permanent position for me. For two years, my job category was referred to as "Surplus to Establishment." But hey, maybe they just forgot. It's a big organization, and people's lives and dreams must slip through the cracks all the time.

Right?

I got the distinct sense that the establishment wanted me out of Ottawa and still begrudged the fact that I'd made the rank of corporal. I was being allowed to stay in Diversity Management, but never with any degree of security or permanency or meaningful responsibility. Years later, I read a comment by a Staffing officer who noted that my non-permanent position was ". . . troubling to all."

Staffing was supposed to create a position for me. But no position was ever created.

To be fair, there were issues I worked on that did have some degree of merit. For example, I worked on the burning issue of RCMP souvenirs. The problem was — and remains — that souvenirs were always of white RCMP officers.

Basically, at the time there were no non-white humans depicted on RCMP souvenirs. If you were looking for a souvenir of a brown-skinned RCMP officer, the only items available in any shade of brown were stuffed bears and beavers. When your black mom and dad went to your graduation ceremony at Depot in Regina, it may well have looked like a nice, diverse group of people all lined up in a row. But when your parents, who may have been East Indian or West Indian or Southeast Asian, went to the souvenir shop to proudly buy a memento that reflected you, they could bring home a stuffed bear or a beaver. Or a white-skinned Mountie doll. And that was it.

Perhaps the most rewarding assignment I undertook in Diversity Management was to have the Visible Minority Advisory Committee (comprised of civilian members) participate in the RCMP's firearms training. These were people who often had never fired a gun. But almost every time that a decision made by a member to use deadly force in the field was brought before them, they would comment, "The assailant was only armed with a knife. Why didn't the member shoot to wound?"

These comments were especially poignant in the context of white cops shooting black persons. I thought that having the committee undergo firearms training would give them insight into some of the realities of policing, because explaining the flaw in this thinking to someone who had never been attacked by a knife-wielding assailant was nearly impossible. You simply can't convince a civilian that you need to put the race of the assailant last and the behaviours of the individual police officer and the person who was shot first. I figured if I could put these civilians into a mock-up situation where they had to decide whether to shoot or not shoot someone, it might change their way of thinking.

The RCMP was resistant at first. But once I explained that I was trying to help committee members understand the physiological and psychological aspects of a deadly force encounter — and that this was the only means available to do so — the idea was accepted. Firearms training put the committee members through a series of shoot/don't shoot scenarios, in which deadly force decisions had to be made in real time. Once the committee members went through the training, they got it. When they saw an image of a man charging at them with a knife, they either shot or they died a virtual death and failed the training. When I subsequently asked them the colour of the man running at them with the knife, none of them knew.

The exercise was viewed as a resounding success. It helped the committee understand the use of deadly force in the officer/violator context, and how to properly undertake follow-up investigations to such incidents. Officer and violator behaviour came first, race came last. The exercise was so much of a success that I was asked by the commissioner of the RCMP to have the same scenario run for the "H" Division, Nova Scotia's Visible Minority Advisory Committee.

While I was languishing at Diversity, in 1995, the Association of Black Law Enforcers (ABLE) was created in Toronto to address black police officers' issues and to mentor black inner-city youth. I joined immediately and later became ABLE's Issues Officer. ABLE is still doing good work in the community and for its membership. Of course, there was an immediate backlash from some white police agencies to the establishment of the group, but we black officers took it all in stride. When some white police officers are threatened when black cops go to dinner together as a group, it wasn't surprising to us that they got scared when we formed our own association.

Despite being relegated to the purgatory of desk duty, protective policing kept creeping back into my life. Those in the force who knew me understood that despite whatever red X had been drawn through my name, I was still an international expert in the field. While my skills might have been immediately put to use in dealing with the intricacies of stuffed animals in red serge at gift shops, I was still approached for consultations.

In 1995, for example, André Dallaire broke into the prime minister's residence at 24 Sussex Drive. Dallaire would later claim that he had heard voices that had instructed him to kill Prime Minister Chrétien. Chrétien's wife, Aline, had to defend herself with a statue against the attacker. Dallaire had been caught on surveillance camera during the initial break-in, and the RCMP's lagging response time to Aline Chrétien's 911 call was interpreted as a national embarrassment. The break and enter was a major breach of security for the nation. People could have been killed, but luckily nobody was injured.

A member from Staffing came to me in Diversity Management for advice on the matter. He asked me some questions, one of which was whether I thought it was appropriate for the prime minister to have shown RCMP members around the residence after Dallaire had been apprehended.

Although Dallaire's break-in appeared to be a single-person event and there didn't seem to be any further danger, security at the prime minister's residence had been breached. Therefore, he and his family should have been immediately taken to a secure site. My response was a firm no.

The other question was where I thought the prime minister should be taken in the event of another security breach. I suggested that a contingency plan be put together for just such a scenario, and that the immediate location should be across the street at the governor general's residence as it was already a secure site.

Around the same time, there had been a shake-up in the PMPD. Groulx was out, and a newly promoted officer had become superintendent. I knew the man and had no problem with him, personally or professionally. He asked to meet with me. In our meeting, he made reference to my extensive knowledge of all aspects of protective policing and asked if I'd come back to train PMPD members.

I replied that if he was resurrecting the training unit that Groulx had ultimately disbanded, then I'd come back full-time in that capacity. His answer was no; I wasn't being invited back into a full-time position, because I didn't speak French. As I understood it, he wanted me to come back with my expertise to instruct the PMPD whenever required, and that I'd provide instruction in English and members would communicate with me in English. But he wouldn't actually hire me because I didn't speak French.

Obviously, I was needed by the PMPD. Their offer was to use me when they needed me. But they wouldn't employ me in a permanent position. The irony was that I still had no permanent position at Diversity Management, where I spent most of my days at a desk booking flights and hotels and making sure committee members had feather pillows.

My answer to the training request was no.

In 1996, there was a need for the RCMP to conduct international training in Grenada, West Indies, on the topic of protective policing and VIP security. My former co-worker, Sergeant MacDonald, who had years ago refused to buckle to pressure and blacklist me from training, was still in the Training Branch. MacDonald approached Dieter Schachhuber to ask that I be allowed to go. I took part in the international training, but afterwards returned to the Diversity Management section, to my regular "duties."

Oddly enough, when I received my annual assessment that year, I was again criticized in writing by my immediate supervisor Sergeant Salh. Again, it was noted that I had exceeded my duties by participating in the training in Grenada. He wrote, "This is not socially acceptable, from a policing perspective." He also wrote negatively about my involvement with black race relations. But I was the race relations advisor! And I was black!

I couldn't win. If I worked to my job description, my assessment was fine. But I had no permanent job and no job description. If I went beyond my duties for the RCMP, upon request, I was criticized. I responded in writing to my assessment, "The RCMP, the Government of Canada, and the Grenadian government find this socially acceptable from a policing perspective."

In 1996, while I was still with Diversity Management, serious conflict again flared up between the black community of North Preston and the RCMP detachment in Cole Harbour, Nova Scotia. According to sources within the force, relations had gotten so bad that the RCMP were going to refuse to go into North Preston.

Diversity Management was contacted for assistance in the matter. At that time, Sergeant Ted Upshaw was the new multicultural advisor. Ted was an old friend and an African Nova Scotian like myself. I was actually on vacation in Nova Scotia visiting friends and family at the time. I received a desperate call from one of the officers in Cole Harbour, looking for advice concerning the escalating conflict between the police and the community. Ted and I were tasked with going to the Cole Harbour detachment and into the surrounding black community. We did ride-alongs with the regular officers on duty, and we went into North Preston to talk with community members about the ongoing issues.

Because I had been around African Nova Scotian communities all my life and had spent eight-and-a-half years with the Halifax Police Department, I had the trust of a lot of people in the black communities. True enough, some of the old resentments lingered. But a fair degree of acceptance was there too. My abilities were also still recognized by the RCMP. Why else would they keep asking me to come back to Nova Scotia to do what they couldn't do?

The only problem was, as with the Halifax Police Department, they wanted the conflicts resolved in their way. When their strong-arm approach didn't work, the best they could do was have a black man attempt to do it for them, in the hopes that the community would accept the ill treatment if "Uncle Tom" offered them the same stale stuff. But black people are not stupid.

As Malcolm X stated, "Sending a Black man into the community in place of a White man to do their bidding is long gone."

Sergeant Upshaw and I fulfilled our mandate and filed a report on the situation. Of course, our mere presence for a few weeks in North Preston didn't solve the problems that had been simmering for generations. But it did manage to break the immediate logjam. There always has been and — until things undergo a radical change — always will be a suspicious and fragile truce between the black community and the police. The issues that have festered and flared up for years have never been dealt with. But remember, it's the police, not the black community, who took the oath to serve and protect. Therefore, the onus is on the police to extend the olive branch and resolve these conflicts.

Back in Ottawa, I felt my mind going numb. Days sitting at my desk, intentionally being given nothing to do, were weighing down on me. It was all too clear that I wasn't wanted there, and that whatever I did was going to be negatively perceived.

To test the waters regarding a transfer out of the nation's capital, I contacted Superintendent Harper Boucher, the commanding officer of the Depot, the training academy in Regina, Saskatchewan. Boucher asked if I would consider becoming an instructor at the Depot. With nothing to lose, I applied and was accepted. And in 1997, I transferred to Regina.

Even this transfer, however, was shady. Instead of being transferred on my merits, I was slotted into an Employment Equity position. This was a position that was supposed to be designated to facilitate the promotion in rank of visible minority members. I was a corporal and was transferred into Depot as a corporal. So in heading to Depot, I took a lateral transfer, but my transfer into an Employment Equity position ate up the actual possibility of a visible minority constable getting a promotion.

CHAPTER 11
CREATING LITTLE CALVINS

The last time I'd been in Depot was 1978. Back then, it was a pressure cooker with different cliques and groups bullying the junior members. Twenty years later, I found it a more collegial, helpful and open environment. Louis Riel's noose was gone from the museum. But the command-and-control environment was still in place. Brainwashing was still the order of the day; now, it was just more refined. The dysfunctional alcoholic family had not changed its composition, nor its debilitating influence on individual cadets and members.

As a new facilitator in the Depot, I was supposed to attend a facilitator's course prior to being assigned a troop of cadets of my own. This course was meant to familiarize new instructors with issues around adult education and training. In familiar fashion, I slipped through the cracks and was never provided with the instructor's course. I was simply dropped into the mix and expected to sink or swim . . . again. I think my exit from Ottawa had been so swift and so heavily

encouraged that mere technicalities — such as actually training me for my new position — were knowingly overlooked.

As I approached this new assignment, I was both excited
and anxious. It was a chance for change. It was a whole new
job. I knew some people at Depot, having either trained
them in VIP or worked with them in the field. There was
even a member from the Halifax Police Department with
whom I'd worked decades ago. In Regina, the toxic situation
with management in Ottawa had not influenced their opinion of me as a quality police officer. But I would have been
naïve to think that they hadn't heard what had gone down.
In the RCMP, there's no such thing as a secret.

A troop consists of between thirty-two and thirty-six
cadets. I and two other facilitators were each assigned our own
troop. I was charged with ensuring that my recruits learned
about aspects of Canadian law, officer deportment, use of
force, as well as anti-harassment and anti-discrimination
policies. These cadets were my responsibility, twenty-four
hours a day. My duties also included being available should
they have any personal or professional problems. If need be,
I could send them to see the psychologist.

I had a lot of authority over the recruits in my troop.
I could provide them with written documentation on
their performance, good or bad. I could recommend their
termination. But I was also their anchor, and my goal was to
see that everyone graduated having mastered the required
course materials. Not everyone did graduate, because police
work is not for everyone. Nothing, aside from training, can
adequately explain what police work is actually about. A
snippet of *Cops* or some similar, sensational police program
on TV is a far cry from the reality of day-to-day policing.
Recruits who showed up with this romantic notion of the job

often had a painful wake-up call — and were often the first to experience an early exit from training.

My facilitation skills, even without the facilitator's course, were above average. Since 1970, when I was with the Halifax Police Department, I'd been lecturing members as well as the general public on a wide range of topics. In the command-and-control environment of the instructional process, I encouraged my cadets to apply critical thinking and responses to whatever on-the-job situations might arise. I challenged them on aspects of the policing process that would have otherwise been applied in a by-the-book fashion. I taught them about the realities of policing. In my classes, if they could articulate the reasons behind an alternate approach to a situation, I'd allow it.

My teaching style was to first provide the rationale for a process, then teach the process itself. If you teach only the process, then yes, you've trained your students. But if you teach the reasoning behind the process, then you've educated them. Rather than being strictly their facilitator, I strove to be my cadets' partner in the training endeavours we undertook. Some facilitators demanded that the cadets come to attention when they walked into the room. But I didn't want any part of this. In my mind, you can't have a positive learning environment with facilitators who place deportment above learning. I taught my recruits that being an RCMP officer was not a cross between being God and Superman, despite what the popular perception might be. I had to walk a fine line here between telling them the reality of the situation — in comparison to the artificial lifestyle being presented all around them — and maintaining order by promoting the official party line. I told the cadets that over the duration of their careers, they would experience different management styles that would vary from democratic to autocratic. Adaptability to rapid change in any situation, no matter the management style or the circumstances, was essential for success.

I couldn't go so far as to tell them that they would watch some of their colleagues become alcoholics, or that some of them in the very room would probably wind up committing suicide due to on-the-job stresses. I did my best to give them a positive outlook for a great career — steeped in reality.

In addition to facilitating, I volunteered for other duties at Depot. I became a member of the Women's Committee, which had been set up to address the workplace-related concerns of female employees and members. As a black officer, I thought that my participation on this committee would be valuable. In my mind, sexist behaviour and racist behaviour are two sides of the same coin. And I had ample experience presenting on — and living with — discriminatory behaviour.

In October 1999, I was the keynote speaker at a Women's Policing Conference at Depot. My speech focused on sexual harassment and discrimination against women that take place in the nine major areas of daily life — economics, education, entertainment, labour, law, politics, religion, sex and war. These are described in Neely Fuller's book *The United Independent Compensatory Code/System/Concept*. Although Fuller's book was geared towards educating black people about surviving in a white supremacist system, it also applies to the discrimination women experience in these major areas of their lives.

For example, women in the RCMP were allegedly being harassed for becoming pregnant. There were stories of detachment commanders making lewd comments such as

"Next time, keep your legs closed!" One of my own female cadets was harassed by her future detachment commander, who commented to her about her breast size.

Allegations of sexual harassment and subsequent payouts by the RCMP — as well as pensions issued by Veterans Affairs Canada because of the mental distress related to these episodes — were, and continue to be, common occurrences. In 2004, for example, the RCMP settled sexual assault allegations against Sergeant Blundell. Four female RCMP officers reported they had been sexually assaulted during undercover assignments with Blundell in charge. But this is just one incident.

As I write this book, there are upwards of four thousand complaints by female members against the RCMP. Each one of these complaints has the potential for major settlements — and Veterans Affairs pensions — to be paid out. Maybe the outstanding bill for these settlements will wake Canadians up to the fact that something is very wrong with the dominant culture in the RCMP.

Relationships between members was another issue I touched on in my speech. Obviously, with members on the force working long hours in close quarters, there was going to be romance and therefore breakups. But in the hyper-masculine climate that permeated the RCMP, sadly these breakups sometimes ended in violence. In June 2001, just after I'd left Depot, Constable Jocelyn Hotte murdered his ex-girlfriend Lucie Gélinas. He emptied two clips from his service pistol into her car. Leading up to the murder, Hotte had had a history of harassment of other female members in the RCMP.

Occasionally, Depot contracted its services out to other federal government agencies. We facilitators were farmed out and used as instructors in various roles and for various topics. Personally, I was approached by the RCMP to design and present a training program for Correctional Services of Canada on the escorting of high-risk inmates. I delivered the presentation to correctional officers at the Saskatchewan Penitentiary in Prince Albert. I tweaked my VIP training to fit the intent of the course. I developed tactics and techniques to protect inmates from potential attack and prevent escape attempts. The session was a success, and I repeated the training several months later.

Throughout my time in Regina, I never gave up my role in police race relations. The force, as usual, was quick to call on me when they needed someone to mop up messes their members had created by exercising racist behaviours. Racial conflict between police officers and the public — and even within the cadet training program itself — continued to rear its festering head.

For example, the Saskatchewan Ministry of Tourism had contacted Depot seeking a cadet in red serge for a promotional poster. According to an email, which was internally circulated at Depot, the provincial Ministry of Tourism had allegedly requested a "white male cadet" for their promo poster. When I read the email, I immediately contacted the sergeant who'd sent it around. I explained to the man that this request was actually totally against RCMP policy, and warned him that this risked becoming a human rights issue.

Despite my attempt to put out this particular fire, someone in Depot sent a copy of the email to the local media. It appeared in the local newspapers a few days later. I spoke to the sergeant once again and advised him to raise the issue immediately with Harper Boucher, our commanding officer. A local First Nations group rightfully took issue with the email and requested a meeting with Boucher. At the meeting, which I attended, the issue was addressed in a spirit of apology, and there was agreement that this would not happen again. Thankfully, it became a teachable moment for everyone involved.

On another occasion, Inspector Keith Clarke, who was in charge of the Applied Police Sciences section at Depot, called me into his office. Clarke wanted to pick my brain about some of my co-workers who had been making racist remarks to the cadets in our facility. The problem, as I saw it, was that there was no policy in place to hold facilitators accountable for their own racist behaviour. All the existing checks and balances simply assumed that racist behaviour would be limited to cadet-on-cadet or cadet-on-facilitator racism. It was expected that the grown men and women in charge of the next generation of RCMP officers would not engage in racist behaviour. But sadly, it happened regularly.

One of my cadets, a young First Nations person, had personally been subjected to racist behaviour by one of his instructors. The driver training facilitator had referred to First Nations people as "wagon burners" and added a few other derogatory remarks to his teachings. I'm sure this type of racist behaviour was traumatic for the cadets towards whom it was directed as well as those within earshot, which included my young cadet. It was all the more distressing because cadets were supposed to be able trust and emulate their supposedly mature instructors.

Needless to say, I ensured that the cadet got justice.

With the passing of years and the thickening of the protective shell in which I'd cloaked myself, I'd forgotten how painful it was to feel the sting of racist behaviour for the first time in the workplace. The confusion, the pain

Calvin with an RCMP troop at the RCMP Training Academy in Regina in 1997.

and the disillusionment one felt, after having been told that there was zero tolerance for harassment and discrimination, made my heart ache — especially when such behaviour came from someone they were supposed to trust with their future. I knew that these young men and women had not yet built up the defence mechanisms to deflect the emotional turmoil and pain. In my experience, sadly, the only recourse was to become numb and develop the emotional scar tissue that came with trying to navigate my own experience within a racist society.

Difficulties between facilitators and cadets were not uncommon. Some facilitators' approaches were perceived as harassment by the cadets under their charge. When cadets filed complaints, it resulted in offending facilitators temporarily being transferred to Program Support while the complaints were investigated. Unfortunately, these investigations happened with enough regularity that it became a sick joke among instructors to see who had undergone their weekly transfer to Program Support.

Further to my conversation with Inspector Clarke, I suggested that the issue of racism should be added to the facilitator's course — the course I'd not been given. Clarke asked if I would speak to the incoming facilitators the next time the course was offered. I agreed.

During my presentation to the next generation of facilitators, one of the incoming facilitators raised his hand and asked, "Shouldn't we call black cadets niggers, so that they know what to expect on the street?"

I swallowed hard. Until that point, my mantra had always been that there's no such thing as a stupid question. I guess that if that type of question was going to be asked, this would be the time and place to do it. I responded that the hypothetical black cadet would probably have been called a nigger before. And that if the facilitator chose to call him a nigger within the confines of a classroom at RCMP Depot, there would likely be negative legal and human rights repercussions.

There was a sergeant on the course who recognized my abilities and gave me a 10-04. A few months later, when another facilitator's course was scheduled, I expected to be called again to give my presentation. Instead, I was told that Depot had hired Reggie Newkirk, a consultant, to do the presentation. I was welcome to come and listen. Newkirk was a black American and a learned man, but he had no RCMP experience and little understanding of the RCMP's culture. I was puzzled as to why Program Support at Depot would bring in an outside person and pay them, when I had proven my ability to do the job. By this point in my career, I was disappointed, but no longer surprised, by anything that the RCMP did.

It was at this time that an interesting opportunity presented itself. I decided to run in the upcoming election to be the sub-representative of the Division Staff Relations Representative (DSRR) system. This system was the RCMP's equivalent of an association that looked after members' issues. Since the RCMP's inception in 1919, members had not been allowed to unionize, and the DSRR was the only mechanism available to us. I won the election unanimously, and, with the assistance of the DSRR, I represented the members at Depot on a number of important issues.

When I was elected as the sub-representative, I'd been at Depot instructing in Applied Police Sciences for approximately three years. An opening came up for a facilitator in Police Defensive Tactics (PDT), someone with fighting skills. In Applied Police Sciences, I was already teaching the philosophy of the use of force, so it seemed like a perfect fit. I applied to PDT, and my boxing training paid off. I was accepted. Now my teaching would all be hands-on.

My time with PDT was one of the most rewarding of my career. Each facilitator had their respective areas of expertise — judo, Muay Thai, grappling, boxing. I was choked by some of the nicest guys you'd ever meet! As I wiped blood from my lip after sparring sessions, I couldn't help but smile at my luck. This was the life. PDT was also responsible for handcuffing techniques, collapsible baton training and pepper spray training. We also ran scenarios to ensure that the cadets made good decisions vis-à-vis their use of force.

Around this time, RCMP Headquarters in Nova Scotia developed a Community Constable program in which people from the Preston areas were recruited to act as community constables. These constables were not RCMP officers, but

Calvin receiving a twenty-year Long Service and Good Conduct Medal in Regina in 1998.

would liaise with the community and the police, acting as a buffer between the two. I was assigned to assist with the training of these community constables when they were sent to Depot. A lot of the trainees were young, but eager to take part in the initiative. I knew some of their families, and I was proud to instruct them on pre-policing procedures.

CHAPTER 12

MAJOR BETRAYAL OF RCMP CORE VALUES

My two years with PDT flew by, and in the fall of 2001, after five years teaching at Depot, Staffing advised me that I was either first or second on the list of officers to be transferred out. Some facilitators transferred out of Depot before the five years, due to promotions or other career moves. However, Depot policy dictated that facilitators were to spend a maximum of five years before being transferred back to their divisions of origin. In my case, this would have been Headquarters and "A" Division in Ottawa.

I wrote to Staffing in Ottawa, alerting them to my imminent transfer. This should have triggered a written response on their part and begun the search for a position for me. Personally, I was ready to return to Ottawa. I'd instructed for five years. I'd done more than my job description at every level. I'd lectured and trained at outside agencies and at universities. I was fifty-two years old and had been a police officer for thirty-two years. I knew I was in the twilight of my career, and I wanted to end on a high note with a new challenge.

I waited for several weeks, but Ottawa didn't acknowledge or respond to my email. The lack of communication set off alarm bells for me, but it wasn't the first time I'd been ignored for no apparent reason.

There were, however, a few lingering procedural issues at Depot that required attention. On the fifth anniversary of my start at Depot, I realized that my annual performance evaluation had not yet been completed for the two years prior. RCMP policy dictated that annual assessments were to be done around the beginning of January each year. Assessments were how RCMP management kept track of the abilities and accomplishments of its members, and, of course, they were integral to any promotional possibilities and positions that the member might apply for.

My assessments were often late because my anniversary date was in January. In this case, however, the delay was unacceptable. I went to my sergeant several times and respectfully requested that I have my assessment completed — to no avail. I then went to the staff sergeant in administration, who assured me that my assessment would be completed.

Several weeks went by, and nothing happened.

Out of frustration, I made an appointment with Superintendent Boucher. I explained my dilemma. Boucher assured me that my assessments would be completed in a timely manner.

I waited another three weeks. I made another appointment with Boucher and requested that he revisit the instructions he had relayed to my sergeant. He was irritated that his instructions had apparently been ignored. By mid-March, my assessment was finally completed to both my and my sergeant's satisfaction. I know of cases where assessments hadn't been done for years. And when the member sought a promotion, or a supervisor attempted to invoke discipline, there was simply no documentation available to support the activity. I also know of members who were told by their supervisors to do their own assessments.

There was also the matter of the facilitator's course, or lack thereof, which came back to haunt me. Because I'd never been given the course, there was no official documentation of my having completed the prerequisites to teach at Depot. In a way, it was as though I had never officially been there. I had to get a certificate made up that stated I had the equivalency of the course, and I had to find a supervisor who was willing to sign off on this makeshift document. It was hardly the proper procedure for entering and subsequently exiting Depot — but such was my career.

Several months went by, and I remained at Depot without any contact from Staffing in Ottawa. Anticipating a realistic timeline for my transfer back to Ottawa was quickly becoming a fantasy. On a bright note, however, after being alone for a long period of time, I had come to grips with my family-of-origin issues. My ability to trust was somewhat improved. I felt that I understood myself better and had a more realistic view of who I was and where I fit as a human being on this planet. Overcoming my long-standing apprehensions of engaging in a personal relationship, I had married.

My wife, in anticipation of a quick move, accepted a job transfer with the federal government and moved herself and our belongings back to Ottawa. I figured it would only be a matter of weeks until I followed her. Now, as the days rolled by, I found myself sleeping on the floor in a sleeping bag in an empty apartment, with nothing more than a TV and a phone.

On October 5, 2001, I was interviewed by Sergeant Rodrigue from "A" Division Staffing in Ottawa. A few weeks later, I received the report on the interview. Although the interview took hours to complete, Rodrigue's report consisted of four or five sentences. His evaluation in no way documented my abilities and achievements with the RCMP. This report was supposed to be a chronology of my career highlights and accomplishments; instead it seemed like everything I had done was being minimized.

I sensed that Rodrigue was afraid of something. Why downplay my lengthy career? Why gloss over an officer's lifetime of service to the force? Diminish my accomplishments. Restrict my opportunities.

Could this be racial tailoring again?

I put together a battle plan.

On November 8, 2001, I received my written confirmation that I was releasable from Depot. During the interim, I'd been keeping tabs on policing job opportunities back in Ottawa, and I was aware that a significant number of members were being sent to the capital as Surplus to Establishment to do enhanced policing duties in the wake of the events of 9/11. With my training in terrorism studies and VIP protection, and my general policing experience, I would have been an asset by any measure. Plus, there would have been no cost associated with my relocation because my wife was already living in Ottawa.

Later in November, having heard nothing from my career manager or anyone else at Staffing in Ottawa, I attempted to contact the section via phone and email. No one responded. No position was offered to me.

Fall turned to winter. I was being blackballed.

On December 11, 2001, I contacted Dieter Schachhuber in the Diversity Management section. I wanted to advise him that I was being prevented from returning to Ottawa. That same day, after enlisting Schachhuber's assistance with my transfer, I received my first response from Staffing. The general message was that everyone was busy, and to please be patient.

On January 2, 2002, still in Regina, I was advised that there were no funds available for transfers until the end of the fiscal year, meaning the end of March. However, in the preceding months, I had watched other corporals at Depot — corporals with later release dates than mine — obtain transfers to other sections. It seemed as though everyone's transfer out of Depot was a fluid process — except for mine.

On January 17, 2002, Dan Pooler, my divisional staff relations member at Depot DSRR, confirmed in an email to me that he had spoken to my career manager, Sergeant Rodrigue. Rodrigue had told him that "there is no money for funding transfers until 01 April 02."

In mid-January, I spoke with a Sergeant from the National Security Investigation section. The Sergeant noted that there were openings in the unit, and that he was willing to take me into his section. I relayed the information to Staffing and Rodrigue.

No answer from Rodrigue was forthcoming. No position was offered to me.

On January 29, 2002, I was sent an email by Sergeant Rodrigue, asking if I'd be interested in taking a position in Executive Diplomatic Protective Services. The job entailed patrolling the embassies in Ottawa, doing uniform duties and any other duties requiring physical security. This was a constable's job, and the understanding was that I would do this job — still as a corporal — until something else was found. Missing my wife and becoming anxious about the entire situation, I accepted the position. Once I accepted, I expected an offer to be made. But no offer was formally made to me.

Around me, I watched constables with one year's service go on to full travel status to fill the staffing gaps in Ottawa. The events of 9/11 had brought huge budgetary increases to the RCMP, and Ottawa in particular was a hotbed of postings. Redeployments to Ottawa were happening all around me.

Yet no position was offered to me.

On February 26, 2002, I was advised by a member at Depot that there were positions available in Ottawa in the National Security Offences section. This job involved working to prevent and investigate threats to national security and internationally protected persons. Keeping in mind that I was told this by a member at Depot — and not by Staffing — I was cautiously optimistic that I might be placed there. On March 7, 2002, after making inquiries, I was advised by Staffing and Personnel that funding for the positions with the National Security section had been cut.

Winter turned to spring. I was still sleeping in my sleeping bag in an empty apartment in Regina. I travelled to Ottawa to visit my wife whenever I could, but I was still stationed at Depot. I had finally let my guard down, finally tried to put down roots of my own. And exactly what I had always feared might transpire had become a reality; my marriage had been geographically split.

With no exit in sight, I continued to teach Police Defensive Tactics at Depot.

In late June 2002, I was assigned to President George W.

Bush's motorcade at the Economic Summit in Kananaskis, Alberta. Although I suspected that I was an untouchable entity in Ottawa, to those members who knew quality VIP policing, I was still valued as an asset in VIP protection.

Emotionally and physically, I was going downhill fast. I was experiencing a major clinical depression. I put on extra weight. My anxiety levels and paranoia paralyzed me. The only emotion left to me was anger, bordering on rage.

Back in Regina, I received a call from the nursing home telling me that my mother in Halifax was dying. The nurse handed the telephone to my mother, and we spoke briefly. She had advanced dementia but seemed to recognize my voice over the line. I caught a flight to Halifax as quickly as I could. When I landed in Toronto to catch the connecting flight, I picked up a phone message; it was staff from the nursing home telling me that my mom had passed away. I didn't make it home to be with her in her final moments. To this day, I wonder, if I had gotten a timely transfer out of Depot back to Ottawa, would I have gotten to Halifax in time to ease her passing?

In tears, I boarded the plane in Toronto and continued back east to make arrangements for her funeral.

Throughout the spring of 2002, the now-standard responses from Staffing continued — there was no money for transfers, I wasn't bilingual, there were no positions available, my investigational experience was dated, and on and on. It seemed as though every day they churned out some new, novel excuse to delay what was rightfully mine.

Mentally and physically, I was completely worn out. I contacted the Depot psychologist for help with my deteriorating mental state. Adding insult to injury, my phone calls were never returned.

Eventually, I was contacted by my career manager. He noted that the officer now in charge of PMPD would be willing to take me back on the team. I would certainly have gone back to PMPD — hell, I never would have left in the first place if given the choice. The only requirement in front of me now was that I had to pass the RCMP physical fitness test, known as PARE, prior to being admitted back onto the PMPD team. In my normal, above-average physical state, I would have passed PARE without a hitch. At that point, however, stuck in Regina, grieving the loss of my mother, missing my wife and having endured six months of on-the-job stress, I had let my fitness level slip. My breath languished, and my heavyweight frame — which I had once used to crush opponents in the boxing ring — was starting to tip scales. I knew I wouldn't pass the PARE test if it was administered.

On the other hand, given what I knew through contacts in Ottawa, I suspected that there were currently members on PMPD who had not passed PARE. All I had to do was find one to confirm my suspicions, then I figured I could take the transfer, get back in fighting form, and pass the PARE test once these devils were off my back. I visited the PMPD in Ottawa and spoke with several members. One of them told me that he had not passed PARE, and that he was going to do it "on his own time."

When I got back to Regina, I contacted Sergeant Gord Hadley in Staffing in Ottawa. I requested that I transfer immediately to PMPD and pass PARE at a later date, as the other member was allowed to do.

Hadley never answered my email. To me, that was it. I had reached the end of my rope. Once again, I donned the now-tired cloak of the angry black man and sought out the services of a lawyer in Regina.

With all the correspondence that I had been sending back and forth over the previous seven months, I had a clear paper trail ripe for the legal picking. I knew that while members in Staffing might not have answered my own emails, I would have inevitably been a hot topic of conversation. It was time to submit one more Access to Information request, this time for all of the emails sent to me by other members, or sent by other members among themselves. The request would provide me with any emails or email threads that mentioned me by name, and several weeks later I received a thick package of very curious emails.

When they finally arrived in May 2002, the emails contained a significant amount of information. Among the emails were damning communications that illuminated the story behind the story; the real reasons why my transfer back to Ottawa had been blocked became crystal clear. The emails painted a picture that showed I was despised by a significant number of RCMP members who had been working in a crude alliance to keep me stalled and languishing in Regina limbo. RCMP managers who had nothing to do with my transfer were copied in emails that had travelled to computers across the country. These included Bev Busson, the commanding officer in British Columbia, where I had never even worked. This well-orchestrated campaign against me was a clear violation of the mission, vision and values set out in the RCMP's employee-related policies.

It was becoming apparent that not only was I blackballed in Ottawa, but I was *persona non grata* throughout the Royal Canadian Mounted Police. As if it were suddenly a break between rounds, I took a step back to my corner to consider my options. For the moment, the lawyer and I kept the emails confidential between us.

As is often the case, once an Access to Information request is filed, the bureaucracy that has been poked with the request reacts after being static. My case was to be no different, and on June 18, 2002, my transfer to Ottawa was approved. I was finally reunited with my wife.

However, due to Hadley's inaction, I had missed my shot at being reunited with the PMPD team. And, as with my waylay in Diversity Management, once I arrived in Ottawa, I was not provided with a section, a position or a contact person to whom I was to report. I had to go find out from Staffing what my job was to be, and who I was supposed to contact.

I'd heard of this tactic before, of "problem" members who'd been sent home and told they'd get a call when there was a position available for them. And there they sat for the rest of their working days. They were never called; they just languished at home, still fit and able to work, and still collecting a paycheque. In my heart, I knew that if I'd just arrived Ottawa, shut up and sat at home, every two weeks I would have received a cheque in the mail, and no one would have ever checked in on me to see where I was or what I was doing.

I made a series of phone calls and was told to report to my new supervisor, Alex Dunn. Dunn immediately suggested that I go full-time on French language training, which had never before been offered to me. There was always a great demand for this type of training. But at this stage in my career, well past fifty years old, what was actually the point of sending me on language training that might have benefitted me twenty years ago? It wasn't a stretch to interpret it as one more attempt to get me out of sight and mind.

When I calmly suggested that French language training might be better used by an officer just starting out in the force, Dunn and his staff suggested that I work as an RCMP fundraiser, operating in conjunction with the United Way. It didn't seem as though they knew what to do with me. Here I was, a policeman with decades of experience and service, being offered everything but police work.

Dunn and his crew finally settled on me working on the Workforce Engagement Wellness Initiative. This was a program established to examine the concerns of the RCMP and the wellness of its members from a cultural perspective. This involved working with Linda Duxbury, who eventually authored the 2017 *Report into Workplace Harassment in the RCMP*. Although I finally had a position, I came to realize that I had become very sick in the process.

There's no warning of the onset of mental ailments such as post-traumatic stress disorder, anxiety or clinical depression. It just comes on bit by bit. You try to manage, but one day it just gets on top of you, and you're no longer who you once were.

I'd spent a lifetime running from emotion. I had always been more comfortable punching the shit out of a bag or a sparring partner than dealing with feelings — but I had run out of gas. Negativity washed over me. To make matters worse, I was being treated as little more than an errand boy in my new job. I'd be sent out to get a book, and when I returned, the supervisor would already have the book in his hand. I was sent to return files to the records office. Nobody cared what I did with my day, and I was being driven mad. My co-workers barely cared if I showed up for work. I had become a glorified gopher with thirty-plus years of experience.

Suddenly, I found myself a potential danger to those around me. I was trained in various martial arts and with numerous weapons, and I was beginning to wonder if I could trust myself to not lash out physically. At that point, I began to worry about my potential to go homicidal at work.

The marginalization and subtle abuse at work wore me down even more. It got to the point that I went to Health Services and attempted to access professional assistance. I showed them the email package I'd received through my Access to Information request and explained my whole story to them. The doctors at Health Services were shocked and dismayed at what they read and heard. They immediately referred me to Dr. André Dessaulles, a clinical psychologist who'd treated many RCMP members in these types of situations. It dawned on me that I had to leave this poisonous work environment before I hurt myself or someone else. I was near my breaking point.

I was placed on sick leave, due to stress. It was supposed to last a few weeks. I went home to recover and regain my balance. I needed to mourn the loss of my career. I needed to mourn the loss of my mother. I found I had never developed techniques to deal with decades of compounded grief. Memories from my entire career began to flood back into the present without invitation or announcement of their arrival.

I couldn't shake the fact that my treatment at the hands of the RCMP had been blatantly unjust, and that I was intentionally being made to suffer. It seemed like this was what happened to a black man who wished to be treated with dignity and respect in the RCMP. My mental state was not the result of my experiences as a police officer. It was due to an internal, co-ordinated attack on me by vindictive members, promoted and endorsed by the RCMP's dysfunctional culture.

Yes, I'd struggled for justice and had publicly called out people who had wronged me. But I had never given the force anything but my best. Now the same members I was expected to trust with my career, and put my life on the line for if need be, seemed intent on killing me slowly.

I could not let that happen.

Just before heading off on sick leave, I filed my second human rights complaint. I had always felt that the Commission was a government tool. Even if you got a settlement, it took years — and it wore you down. But at the point, it seemed like the only option open to me. It was that or fade away towards an early grave without even a whimper to bring attention to my exit.

CHAPTER 13

STAND UP OR BOW OUT

I went home a broken, mentally unwell, disillusioned man. All my plans, my dreams and my work had seemingly been for nothing. It was as though all the energy I'd put into my career had turned on me and was now making me sick. All I'd ever wanted was a meaningful life for myself and my community.

I had heard of and seen police officers who'd gone through what I was going through and who were in the same shape as me. I also knew that many of them ended up dead. I never thought, though, that I'd be one of them. I thought my hard work and respect for others would keep me safe in the workplace even if I had to fight for my causes. I thought that my size and stature and upbringing would keep me immune from it. Now, it became a struggle to get out of bed in the morning. I could've lain there, with the curtains drawn, wearing the same clothes for days. I'd given up on myself. Depression weighed heavily on me.

Like a boxer who's been knocked down, I took an eight count and performed an assessment of my condition. I knew I couldn't stay down like this. I couldn't end my career this way. My self-confidence and self-esteem were destroyed. Deeper than that, though, at my core, I felt a combination of shame, fear and anger. I could gradually feel my last emotion — rage — rearing its tired head. It let it wash over me. It became my fuel.

I was once an outgoing and jovial guy. I would talk to anyone on the street and treat them with humility and kindness. Now, hardened in my shell, I trusted no one and stayed away from almost everyone. I was so angry, I isolated myself out of fear that I might do something irrational. As Dr. Dessaulles told me repeatedly, I had gone through a "personal 9/11 attack." He told me that he didn't want to read about me in the newspaper having committed some kind of horrific violence.

I went to the RCMP physician for medication for my crippling depression and for help with sleeping. The effects of the medication for depression were never monitored with follow-up appointments, which the RCMP doctor should've conducted. The meds made me feel like a zombie. I took the sleeping pills to quiet my mind; otherwise, I couldn't calm down at night. I treated the RCMP doctor as my personal drug dealer, nothing more.

I occupied my days walking dogs for the SPCA. I took a djembe drumming class. I contacted the media, but the responses ranged from frostiness to outright ignoring. I made appointments to see black members of parliament and the senate. Jean Augustine, then a member of parliament for Etobicoke-Lakeshore, wrote that my case was beyond the scope of her position. Senator Ann Cools, the first black Canadian senator, wrote that she was too busy with other issues. Senator Donald Oliver, from the black community in Nova Scotia, wrote a letter to RCMP Commissioner Zaccardelli, advocating on my behalf. In response, Commissioner Zaccardelli advised Senator Oliver that the RCMP Multicultural Advisor of the Diversity Management section was looking into my file. As a result of an Access to Information request that I had previously submitted, the RCMP provided me with a copy of an unclassified memo, dated 2002-06-20. The memo noted that Commissioner Zaccardelli was requesting briefing notes on my ongoing situation.

Diversity Management, one more time.

I emailed Sergeant Yarinder Brar, then the only multicultural advisor in Diversity Management. On July 22, 2003, he responded, "I can tell you that I have never been asked to review any file relating to your complaint." I brought this back to the attention of Senator Oliver, but there was no further response.

On my behalf and at my request, another letter was sent to Commissioner Zaccardelli by the Association of Black Law Enforcers (ABLE), requesting a "comprehensive review of the available information" on my file. Again, there was no response.

I contacted numerous members of then Prime Minister Paul Martin's cabinet, including the Minister of Canadian Heritage Sheila Copps, Solicitor General Wayne Easter and the Minister of Public Safety and Emergency Preparedness Anne McLellan. Each assured me that my complaint was the purview of the RCMP, who would be looking into my case in due time. They did not involve themselves or their respective departments, and no assistance was offered to me.

I was handed back over to the wolves.

I can only surmise that I was being offered up as collateral damage in the overall protection of the image of that national icon, the glorious RCMP. After all, how could there be racist behaviour, if policy forbade it?

During my sick leave, I continued on as the Issues Officer at ABLE. In this capacity, I helped law enforcement officers from across Canada who were dealing with racial abuse at the hands of their employers. My depression had made me like a fighter with a broken hand; I could still hit, but every action shot pain through me.

My self-advocacy was making news through grass-roots policing channels. As the details of my own case became more widely known, officers of all races and genders began to contact me, to tell me their stories. I'd meet them in coffee shops and in parks, and some would break down in front of me as they recounted their painful circumstances. I became an advocate for police officers who were experiencing racial and other forms of abuse. Even if my own life path felt derailed, it gave me a measure of strength to still feel useful.

Ali Tahmourpour's lawyer approached me about instances of racism that had taken place at Depot in Regina. Tahmourpour was a cadet who had had his contract terminated, and who had subsequently launched a human rights complaint. I was a facilitator at Depot at the time of his termination, but he was not one of my troop, and at the time I hadn't been aware of his situation. At the request of his lawyer, I was called upon to provide evidence at the tribunal hearing concerning systemic racist behaviour in the RCMP, including for the time period when Tahmourpour and I were both at Depot. This tribunal took place in 2000.

It took ten years for that case to work its way through to the federal Court of Appeal, but in July 2010, the court found that the RCMP had discriminated against Tahmourpour on the basis of race and religion. I was peripherally happy for him, and for having played a part in his vindication.

However, I was not looking forward to my own ten-year-long court battle. In my darker hours, now no longer a young man, I figured I'd die or be rendered mentally incapacitated before my case ever saw legal light. Although I was skeptical of the human rights complaint process, given my past experience with this system, I knew I had enough evidence to show that the RCMP had acted in bad faith in dealing with my transfer and treatment.

I'd let my communications lag with my lawyer in Regina, so I approached David Yazbeck, a labour relations lawyer based out of Ottawa, for legal representation. Letting my pent-up rage fuel my actions, I brought Yazbeck the emails I'd received through my Access to Information request. Laid bare in front of him, Yazbeck began to understand the web of deceit and cover-ups that formed the basis of proof for my complaint, and the damning paper trail I had kept close to my chest as a final, third-round flurry. I had evidence of a cover-up.

Chronologically, the story, as per my request emails, goes as follows:

On October 3, 2001, my career manager, Sergeant Michel Rodrigue, spoke with Yves Rainville, a member of Staffing in Ottawa "A" Division. As my career manager, Rodrigue's priority should have been finding me an appropriate placement back in Ottawa, my division of origin prior to being outsourced to Depot in Regina. This, however, does not appear to have been the case. In this first email in my request package, Rodrigue wrote to Rainville that the commanding officer of "A" Division was curious about whether I was a good candidate for a transfer. Rather than endorsing me as the quality police officer that I was, Rainville replied that I "had a bit of a history — he was on PMPD before and from what I hear, he may not be what we are looking for at this time."

The date of October 3 is important because Sergeant Rodrigue — the man in the driver's seat of my career placement at this point — didn't conduct his transfer interview with me until October 5, two days after Rainville's response to his query. It appears that Rodrigue had been pre-emptively instructed by Rainville that I wasn't what they were "looking for at this time" prior to my interview. It's not surprising to me then that Rodrigue's assessment of my career after the October 5 interview, which took hours to conduct and spanned my entire career, was limited to a few terse lines.

From my request package, it appears that there was silence between this first October email and a subsequent flurry of emails that began in early March 2002. I interpret this lull in email chatter as a stalling tactic; during this period, I was becoming increasingly stressed over the proverbial radio silence surrounding my career placement. Yet for the interim five months, those in charge of my placement appeared to have done absolutely nothing towards helping me transfer back to Ottawa.

As I've explained, however, I did not sit quietly in Regina during this period — indeed, quite the opposite. I had hired a lawyer and put the RCMP on notice. My case was becoming publicly embarrassing for the force. I was making a lot of people, inside and outside the organization, privy to my treatment. In apparent response, various Staffing departments and implicated sections in Ottawa were forced to open an email dialogue to address my transfer — or lack thereof.

The next email in my request package was dated March 7, 2002, from Dan Pooler, my DSRR at Depot in Regina, to Michel Rodrigue. In the email, Pooler wrote, "Thanks for the update. I'll try and keep Cal off your back."

To me, this was a shocking twist. Pooler's role as DSRR was supposed to be limited to ensuring that all of my rights as a member of the RCMP were adhered to, consistent with the mission, vision and values of the organization. Lacking a union of our own, Pooler was supposed to advocate for the proper treatment of members — myself included — in relation to management. I had even worked with Pooler personally when I was a sub-representative at Depot.

In regards to my own case, I had approached Pooler for assistance in facilitating my transfer back to Ottawa and had asked him to monitor and intervene in my situation when and if he felt I wasn't being treated properly. Pooler was supposed to represent *me*, not Staffing in Ottawa. The words in this email, "I'll try and keep Cal off your back," felt like a sucker punch. They told me that Pooler did not have my best interests at heart.

As an aside, years later, when I was mentally debilitated and on sick leave in Ottawa, I was subsequently contacted by a team of lawyers in Toronto regarding RCMP members' attempts to unionize. These lawyers were looking for examples of the failure of the DSRR model to properly represent its members. At the lawyers' expense, I was brought to Toronto to provide them with an affidavit. The lawyer I spoke with was interested in the context and content of this particular email. At the end of our conversation, he told me, "the RCMP lawyers are not going to want to touch you in their rebuttal of your affidavit, because you're the only one that has the division representative failing to represent a member in writing." I'm confident my affidavit contributed significantly to the eventual success of the RCMP members' attempts to unionize.

The next email in my package was from April 9, 2002. Bear in mind that it was now *six months* after my initial interview with Rodrigue, and that during those six months I had watched a number of my co-workers receive their respective transfers. This email was from Sergeant Gord Hadley of Staffing and Personnel in Ottawa to John Spice, the officer in charge of the Ethics Advisory Office. I had approached Hadley with an email request to join the Ethics Advisory Office. I also knew Hadley from my time in PMPD.

It was very troubling to read Hadley's email description of me to Spice, which included a comment on my race. Hadley wrote: "Cpl. Lawrence is a non-White member from N.S." I found this extremely problematic because there were no racial criteria for staffing in the Ethics Advisory Office. Once again, it appeared as though my race could not be separated from my existence as a member of the RCMP.

In this very same email, Hadley wrote: "If you would require additional information on his capabilities, Mr. Dieter Schachhuber, Diversity Management, would be one source/reference."

To me, the mention of Schachhuber was puzzling. I hadn't worked in Diversity Management or under Schachhuber since 1997, and Hadley's email was composed in April of 2002. The proper procedure for Hadley and Spice to have followed to determine whether I was capable of working in the Ethics Advisory Office would have been to interview me and review my file, including my annual assessments. Neither Schachhuber nor Diversity Management had anything to do with this possible transfer — or this process. While I'm fairly sure that Schachhuber would have had nothing but endorsements, this whole process smacked of haphazard and differential treatment.

The next email was from April 18, 2002. It was an email sent out by Sergeant Hadley to two mailing lists, "RM/A" and "RM/HQ," with my name in the subject line of the email. Hadley's email should only have gone out to RCMP members involved in Staffing in "A" Division and Headquarters. Sending out an email concerning me to a vast number of email addresses was completely against RCMP policy. In this email, Hadley wrote that, "we all must continue (where feasible) to try and identify a valid, vacant, and permanent position for the c/n member." Personally, I questioned what the need was for an unnecessarily dispersed email reminding the recipients that I had a right to return to Ottawa. Shouldn't my timely transfer and return have simply been part of the due process?

The next email was from April 19, 2002. In it, Yves Rainville replied to Hadley's email from the day before. Rainville wrote: "There are no opportunities in 'A' Div. Prot. Ops for this member." Although this email chain was already suspect, Rainville further copied twelve other members of Staffing in his response to Hadley, including my career manager, Michel Rodrigue. These twelve members in Staffing had nothing to do with Protective Operations. I understood Rainville's email as a clear message that I was being blackballed across the board, and that no one who had been copied should make any efforts towards bringing me back to Ottawa.

The next email was dated April 28, 2002. In it, Lynn Twardosky, the commanding officer at Depot, wrote to Philip Campbell, a member of Staffing in Ottawa.

Twardosky wrote:

> "*I am sure you are working on it* and not knowing what the real issue is *I have the sense that the more he hears there are vacancies in Ottawa the more likely he is to take legal action.*" (*emphasis added*)

The phrase "not knowing what the real issue is" was, to me, a red flag. If the *real issue* was not finding me a suitable permanent position, as per Sergeant's Hadley earlier email, then what exactly was it? This particular email also confirmed to me that there were indeed vacancies in Ottawa, vacancies that should have — but were not — being offered to me. Rather than those vacancies being made available to me, Twardosky's concern was that I would find out about them!

My request package further provided me with what appeared to be the handwritten synopsis of a voicemail message left on April 30, 2002, concerning John Spice. Although no name is attributed to the voicemail, the initials M.S. suggest the synopsis was written by Mike Seguin, the Director General of Staffing and Manager Relations in Ottawa. Seguin's name appears in my request package on many other occasions. The voicemail message reads as follows:

> [*John Spice*] *had dealt with Staffing to have Cal work there* but was unaware of the whole issue. *He is going out to Regina and will be meeting*

with him. It was made clear that my call was not
to influence his decision on staffing his own area
but simply to have him aware of the situation
so that a solution beneficial to Cal and the RCMP
is found. (emphasis added)

John Spice never once spoke to me in Regina. I had
certainly been interested in being transferred to the Ethics
Advisory Office, where Spice was the officer in charge. To
me, the use of phrases such as "unaware of the whole issue"
and "have him aware of the situation" suggested an active,
co-ordinated attempt to keep from getting any meaningful opportunities in Ottawa. From the email, it appeared as
though Spice himself had initially been interested in accepting
my request for transfer to his section. When the time came
for this possibility to be enacted, certain individuals appear to
have made concerted efforts to block it.

The next email in my request package was dated May 7,
2002. In it, Sergeant Hadley wrote to Lynn Twardosky:

Cal isn't the only expert in VIP duties, the force
has plenty of those.

He then added:

"I know he tries to sell himself to managers but
maybe he's trying too hard. I know (all the career
counsellors in this shop know VERY WELL) how
demanding the managers in HQ are. They usually
get what they need and want. Cal is not what
they need/want." *(emphasis added)*

I was surprised, but at this point no longer shocked by anything I read in my request package. After working and dedicating my life to VIP topics and duties, for Hadley to say that I was just one of a bunch of available experts was inaccurate and hurtful. It also, once again, went against the core values of the Royal Canadian Mounted Police.

As far as not being wanted or needed in Ottawa, with the staffing shortages brought about by the Twin Tower bombings in 2001, my skill set was definitely in need. However, Sergeant Hadley's words clearly show that not being wanted took precedent over being needed. Canadian citizens and other RCMP members would have benefitted from having me in Ottawa. Instead, constables with one or two years experience were hired ahead of me. It appeared as though the RCMP would rather jeopardize the security of the country than have a black man who's challenged the system in town. They refused to bring in one of the best, the brightest and the most experienced to provide security for this country.

CHAPTER 14
INTEGRITY INTACT

As my human rights complaint worked its way through the system, mediation was suggested to me at every stage. To have a Human Rights Tribunal actually take place would have meant huge investments of time, money and stress. It would be years before my case was adjudicated, and even then, they might not find in my favour.

In the interim, as my case slowly plodded along, I filed another Access to Information request. In it, I found out, through internal emails, that the RCMP had put fifty thousand dollars aside — to start — as a war chest to legally deal with my case. At this stage of my life, I didn't need the pressure of a prolonged court battle, nor did I have the finances to match the RCMP's pockets. I also knew that the years of stress would bury me.

I agreed to the mediation process, as did the RCMP.

In the midst of the process, then-Chief Superintendent Fraser MacAulay was playing a major role in the negotiations as a representative of the force. During our mediation talks, thanks to information provided to me by a friendly insider I knew within the force, it came to my attention — and surprise — that MacAulay was himself the subject of a recent racial discrimination complaint. This sent me into a mental tailspin; I went into total panic mode.

Here was MacAulay, ostensibly meant to resolve my case in an honourable manner, consistent with the core values of the RCMP. I wondered how he could do this, from an ethical and moral standpoint, if he himself was the subject of a racial discrimination complaint. I thought that my own negotiations would be compromised with MacAulay dealing with me on behalf of the RCMP. In my opinion, he should have recused himself from my mediation process. But it was not to be.

On November 4, 2003, after I had undergone numerous mediation sessions and meetings with teams of lawyers, a settlement finally appeared to be close at hand. At that point I was called in by then–RCMP Assistant Commissioner Vern White. He offered me a position with a new project called Bridging the Gap, which was supposedly meant to train up community program officers as intermediaries between the RCMP and various at-risk communities. These community representatives wouldn't be RCMP officers, but would provide some form of by-community policing. As White explained it to me, I would be part of the roll-out process of this initiative. I told him that I was involved in ongoing mediation, and that after months, my team and I were very close to a settlement. I respectfully declined his offer.

Without my consent or knowledge, White then inserted himself into the mediation process by contacting the RCMP mediator and the force's legal team. I'm not privy to what White said to the mediator and the lawyer, but whatever was said completely derailed the carefully negotiated agreement we had nearly arrived at. The potential agreement was swiftly taken off the table.

My options suddenly became limited to either accepting White's supposed job offer or starting all over with the mediation process. This would mean further months and years of fighting the RCMP and their deep pockets in a tribunal. Reluctantly, without options, I accepted White's proposal. But there was never any follow-up to this job offer. No one contacted me to make arrangements to be placed in the hypothetical Bridging the Gap position. It was yet another empty promise and process. I was being toyed with. But it had the effect of ending my mediation process. In my mind, that was the only intended impact.

Curious, I filed yet another Access to Information request, specifically related to Vern White's self-insertion into my mediation process. I subsequently found that on November 14, 2003, Vern White sent an email to Deputy Commissioner Barbara George. In it, White wrote:

> *I suggest we order him to the job identified with Suzanne, if he refuses we start admin. discharge procedures for failing to follow, his complaints are separate from the work offered.*

Vern White — now a Canadian Senator — never informed me that my administrative discharge was on the table if I didn't take his supposed job offer. It's astounding to me that not only did White directly intervene in my mediation process, but he and others would have seen no problem in giving me an ultimatum-style, "take it or leave it" job offer, which, in emails, had my termination attached to it if I didn't accept. And remember, all of these machinations were taking place while I was already on sick leave due to the mental stress inflicted upon me by the RCMP.

That's kicking a man when he's down. That's the lowest of the low.

And where is Vern White now?

Sitting in the Canadian Senate.

In a stroke of luck, I had a passing conversation with the head of the RCMP's Access to Information and Privacy (ATIP) section. Although my interpretive skills had been frayed, I sensed that the department head knew that I'd been screwed over and was empathetic to how the system had ground me down. He reached out to Staffing and said that there was a position available for me at the ATIP office. Thinking back on it now, with the amount of sensitive and confidential information passing through my fingertips on a daily basis, the ATIP office was probably the very last place that the RCMP managers wanted me after what they'd done.

At ATIP, I was like a kid in a candy store. My job there involved vetting requests for information. I'd sit in front of the computer, read files and determine what was releasable and what was protected information, based on the *Access to Information Act*. I was subsequently transferred into the policy section of ATIP. Even though it was desk work, sifting and sorting through requests for information, I was useful again.

The problem was, by this point, I'd been off work on sick leave for over two years. Because of my notoriety over the case, a significant number of members gave me the cold shoulder. Mentally, I had never felt this fragile in my life. Every look, every muttered word, which used to just wash over me, cut me to my core. I used to walk the Saturday night streets with a sense of pride in my job, impervious to the catcalls and racist taunts. Now, sometimes I couldn't even look my co-workers in the eye.

My psychologist, Dr. Dessaulles, had warned me that when I returned to work, it would be a whole different dance, a whole different feeling and a whole different language. In his office, when he described the mistrust I would feel in the work environment, I doubted his words. Ultimately, though, he was right. It was like I had just undergone major surgery; every step was taken gingerly.

I was trying to sift through the pieces of my career and make a comeback, but nothing felt the same. My trust in the system — in the glorious red serge — was gone. I was experiencing clinical paranoia, and it affected my ability to trust others. My medication numbed the symptoms, but, stuck in the toxic environment that had rendered me ill, I thought I was the topic of every conversation. I heard my name whispered around every corner. Trying to interpret who was for me and who was against me occupied a great deal of my energy — and it exhausted me.

Numbed now, I felt that I could have easily have taken any one of my co-workers out back behind the office and put a bullet in their head. All I'd have felt was the recoil of the gun in my hand. And I would've just disposed of the body, gone back to work and eaten my lunch. I was edging towards homicidal, and what frightened me most was that I had been given the skill set to plausibly commit murder.

You can't get well in the place that made you sick. It wasn't healthy for me or for anyone around me. For the sake of myself and my family, I knew it was best to retire. I had taken my body and my mind to the edge. I had done the best I could for as long as I could. I had fulfilled my role as a police officer and a Canadian citizen. It was time to go.

Grudgingly, I reached a settlement with the RCMP. Not doing so would have dragged the process out for years. The terms of the settlement are confidential, and for me to divulge its contents would result in an RCMP lawsuit. One of the pitfalls of these types of mediations, which are not uncommon, is that the public is kept in the dark about the financial agreements and other concessions made. In my opinion, if the public knew, there would be an immediate and extreme backlash. I was mentally destroyed on the public's dime. And I was paid out and shuffled off — again on the public's dime — once the system reduced me to a nonfunctioning shell of my former self.

Because of what I had gone through, I supplied all my documentation — including all my Access requests — to Veterans Affairs Canada. I applied for a medical pension because of my clinical depression. The doctors at Veterans Affairs agreed that I was suffering. Veterans Affairs Canada stated that I'd been subjected to "exceptional service-related stress and that this stress resulted in the development of . . . major depression." I want you, the reader, to note that my depression was not caused by incidents related to my policing duties. It was caused by abuse perpetrated by people who I was supposed to work for and trust. While no one, including myself, could ever live up 100 per cent to the core values of the RCMP, I felt that the entire organization, as well as certain individuals within it, weren't even going in the right direction.

The push to retire from the RCMP came when I received my Veterans Affairs Canada pension. I calculated my pension based on my age and my years of service in policing (thirty-six), and I decided to retire.

I considered it a policing job well done. I had become an expert in my chosen field of protective policing. I had fought for myself. And I had fought and advocated for others, against a system of white supremacist behaviour. I didn't undo it. I didn't even make it blink. But we found salve to our suffering through community — a community of minorities who felt that their calling was to serve their respective communities through policing.

I submitted my documents to resign. The ATIP section took me out for a retirement dinner. The last day of work, I walked around the building and reflected on my career. I turned in my pass and left the building for the last time.

I retired with an immaculate record with two police agencies, and with a twenty-five-year and a twenty-year good conduct medal from the RCMP.

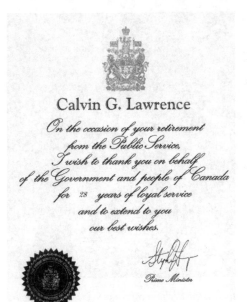

Letter of Appreciation to Corporal Calvin Lawrence from Prime Minister Stephen Harper, received May 8, 2007.

Calvin with RCMP Commissioner Zaccardelli, receiving a twenty-five year Long Service Good Conduct Medal in Ottawa in 2006.

EPILOGUE

Slowly, tentatively, I've come back into myself after dealing with debilitating mental illness. I can smile again. I can bounce my wife's grandchildren on my knee and play with the family dog. I can appreciate the fragility and beauty of life.

I'm now sixty-nine years old. I spent the best part of my life as a police officer. My mindset will always be that of a police officer. I'm grateful that I've been able to enjoy twelve years of retirement because some of my colleagues and friends never even made it to their pensions before they passed on. When I walk down the street, I still have a critical eye for suspicious behaviour. My ability to read people and the streets will never leave me. And because of my life experiences, I've become a much more empathetic person.

I'm grateful that my heart is not filled with hate and bitterness, because I could have easily gone that way. I've relearned how to look for the best in people, no matter what race or gender they are. And I'm grateful when I find it. But I'm also prepared to deal with any kind of abuse that comes at me, racial or otherwise. I'm older now, so I have to pick my causes. I can't take on every injustice that I come across, but people still call on me for help.

I live in a changing world where some of my ideas are viewed as obsolete. Younger people know the rules, but older people know the exceptions. I still swat at a punching bag to deal with my stress. The punches are not as hard as they once were, and they are less frequent. Maybe it's a sign of age.

Perhaps it's a sign that some of my rage has finally left me.

There are some who ask why I ever became a police officer. I answer, because I had a right to. I believed — and I still do — that my community was better served by me in a uniform than by a racist white cop. I had an opportunity thrown in my lap, and I ran with it and made the best of it that I could.

Unless black people plan to sit on their doorsteps all their lives, they will encounter racist and white supremacist behaviour, whatever their endeavours. That's the way life goes. I didn't create it. And I won't see the end of it before I leave this earth. The critical thing is to have the tools to deal with these attacks on our integrity, so that my mistakes are not repeated by those who can learn from them.

I've lectured to anyone who will lend me an ear. I still speak at universities and talk to police agencies who are willing to have me. I speak on police race relations. And I help people who are being abused by an unjust system. As they say in boxing, "You either stand up and be counted, or lie down and be counted out."

As for the policing system I am leaving behind me, I feel that it has deteriorated, generally, due to the lack of officer-citizen contact. I've watched this contact be replaced by technology and a general lack of interest by a significant number of police organizations towards obtaining results through verbal intervention. What policing started out as, as laid out in Sir Robert Peel's principles of policing, was a relationship in which the people are the police, and the police are the people. Police officers should work with the community, for the betterment of the community, from a law enforcement standpoint. I have never swayed from the belief that this should be any police force's singular goal.

Unfortunately, it appears as though police officers today feel they have no obligation to gain the public's co-operation by talking to them. Oftentimes, due to austerity measures that have gutted our mental health safety nets, the people that today's cops are dealing with are mentally ill. Oftentimes, they are angry. It is up to the officer who has taken the oath to serve and protect, to not respond in kind.

To me, sadly, today's police officers would rather show their power than obtain peaceful compliance from the community they are sworn to serve. Coupled with a militarization of police forces and an increased reliance on technology, rather than communication, they are seen as more and more unapproachable by the public. Today's public is understandably afraid of cops. And that's the bottom line.

The answer to today's problems between police and the communities they serve is rooted in the lack of communications training by police organizations, which is more important today than ever before. People today are wrapped up in their cell phones, computers and their technology. Police today fail to understand the importance of being able to communicate with the public and are never taught how to understand or undertake face-to-face interactions in any meaningful regard.

Police officers need to be able to slow their interactions down to the point where the average citizen can understand what they're trying to communicate, particularly in regard to that individual's behaviour from a law enforcement standpoint.

What I'm saying is not novel or new. There are a number of courses and institutions that train police officers on how to do this. Police officers have gotten caught up in the immediacy of their situation.

"We have to do this right away."

The RCMP was built on command and control. That has never changed. No matter what the policies are, no matter what the core values say. Command and control has always been the dominant ideology, both within and outside the organization. There is no "back in my day, it was better" or "it was different when I was around."

The only reason we appear to be seeing more examples of dysfunction crop up these days is because our communications technology has circumvented the established filters and means of censorship that once dominated our news feeds. Technology allows us to communicate the abuse quicker than ever. But despite seeing the abuse play out, the people who have the power to make change do not have the will. Politicians, other officers and in some cases the media are complicit in this.

Personally, I find the media very hesitant to criticize the RCMP, especially when it comes to examples of racist behaviour. Allegations of racism within the RCMP get wrapped up in headlines of bullying, harassment and sexual harassment. It's as though we are all, as Canadians, frightened of the repercussions of criticizing the vaunted RCMP; as though the red serge were a defining icon of the experience of being Canadian.

To change the RCMP, you'd have to change the process of how cadets are indoctrinated. That means you'd have to stop sending people out to Regina. You'd have to stop sending young minds out to be subjected to a process that you'd find being applied in any typical cult-style situation. You'd have to stop breaking down cadets. Stop hazing them and making them feel helpless. Stop reducing them to nothing, only to build them back up in a manner that is unrealistic and creates fear of thinking outside the organizational box.

This could be accomplished by having training centres established around the country, letting cadets go home on the weekends if they wish to do so. The entire system doesn't necessarily need to be destroyed, but higher officers have to relinquish their command-and-control mentality. Accountability measures need to be implemented from the top down.

People do what they think they can get away with. To make the RCMP accountable, it needs to come from the top rank on down. You don't do your job, you lose your rank. And that goes for the commissioner too. The RCMP needs to be a stand-alone organization. The commissioner cannot be a ministerial appointment, appointed via political favour.

The commissioner of the RCMP, at the moment, is a political position, which means he or she is susceptible to the whims of politics. There has to be a break between the government and the commissioner. The commissioner should not be looking over his shoulder to see what his political masters are going to say about the decisions he makes.

In my mind, none of this is going to change until the public realizes that the dominant culture in the RCMP is controlled by white males. They will not give up that dominance to any other culture, whether it be women or non-white people. If there is a threat that they will lose that dominance, it doesn't matter what the laws are. It doesn't matter what the policy says. And it doesn't matter what politicians say. That's the way it is.

I believe that we as black people have no power because we do not organize. Movements like Black Lives Matter, for example, are simply repeating the past reactions to white supremacist behaviour by demanding that we be included as an equal in society. Without the economic and political clout that other groups have, black organizations and black people, for that matter, will simply be ignored. Many young, black organizers have fallen into the trap of taking their problem to the problem, rather than improving their lot as was done historically in 'Black Wall Street' and other examples of self-sufficient black communities.

Women are gaining power through organization and turning their efforts inwards. French Canadians have galvanized their power base. They make a fist out of their fingers. We as black people, in my opinion because of assimilation fantasies, have not organized. Because we have no power, we are susceptible to being treated at the whim of any other culture. The more economic and political power a culture has, the more gains they will make in obtaining that multicultural environment, in all ranks and all organizations, including the RCMP.

We as black people have so much trouble organizing because we are the only culture that can't write that letter back home. Every other culture has a land base and a language. Ours was destroyed through slavery. But today, in my opinion, we should have enough knowledge to know we cannot afford to have conflict with each other. Other cultures can, to a degree. We cannot afford to put all our faith in the dominant European culture and believe that someday we will achieve equality. History, up to the present day, has shown otherwise. We can no longer take our problem to the problem.

APPENDIX

You might be tempted to read this book and write off my story as an isolated incident, or excuse the racist behaviour perpetrated by a few members of the RCMP as not representative of the whole organization. You might brush it aside as a product of a different time, or a specific location. You might hesitate to form any opinions about such a venerable Canadian organization based on one man's experiences.

The RCMP has a long and storied history, and part of that story is how it has acted towards non-white members and citizens across the country, across the decades. The incidents I present here, gathered both during my time in the RCMP and through research, tell that story. They present a pattern of racist behaviour and attitudes. I urge you to read with an open mind.

Incidents in Profile

1941, Nova Scotia

The Sydney Sub-Division of Nova Scotia's "H" Division received an application from two eligible men, Leslie Bryan and Alfred Coward. In a memo to the commanding officer in Halifax dated October 20, 1941, Inspector F.T. Evens requested input into how to handle these applications from the two "coloured men." The commanding officer in Halifax forwarded the request to Ottawa, with a note asking for advice on how this "problem" had been dealt with in other divisions. The Commissioner in Ottawa directed that the men should be given the chance to write the educational test, "with the hope that we shall find that they have not successfully passed." The Commissioner explained that "to definitely refuse them the opportunity of applying on account of their colour would raise the question of policy." He directed that the tests be forwarded for the Commissioner to examine himself before the men were contacted. It is clear in this response that the unofficial policy was to not entertain these applications by any means possible.

Inspector F.T. Evens, Sydney Sub-Division, memorandum, 1941, in the author's possession.
Inspector J.W. Kempston, "H" Division, memorandum, 1941, in the author's possession.
Superintendent F.A. Blake, RCMP Headquarters, memorandum, 1941, in the author's possession.

1961, British Columbia

Charney Biln, a twenty-one year old Sikh man from British Columbia, had successfully written his exams and interviewed in application to become a member of the RCMP. In a memo dated April 25, 1961,

Superintendent G.R. Engel wrote that Biln had been recommended, but that "because of the fact that he is of Indian origin . . . belongs to the Sikh religion and possesses the dark complexion common to his racial group, you may wish to refer this file to the Commissioner for his comments and feelings toward engagement of a person whose race is other than white." This time the response from Ottawa was to engage Biln if he was found suitable, with the additional request that if he were successful, "I wish to be advised as it is the Commissioner's intention to inform our Minister of this engagement, which, in a way would be a departure from ordinary procedure." This illustrates that hiring non-white members was still very much outside the norm, and that these members were not treated in the same way as their white peers.

Patricia Parker, "Charney Biln: The RCMP's First Sikh Member," 1941, Library and Archives Canada, in the author's possession.

1969, Saskatchewan

Ex-corporal Jack Ramsay wrote a scathing article in *Maclean's* describing his fourteen years in the RCMP. Ramsay, a white officer, noted how the culture of the RCMP favoured image and politics over policing or work-ing with communities to improve conditions. In 1969, Ramsay reported his concerns about escalating alcohol abuse and violence in Deschambault, Saskatchewan. Deschambault and Sandy Bay, both remote First Nations villages, could only be reach by air. The nearest RCMP aircraft, in Prince Albert, was only available once every three weeks at best. Ramsay requested permission to charter the aircraft more often in an effort to build community ties and work to prevent more serious violence. He was denied, with the reasoning that this would cost too much. He was, however, permitted to charter in to Sandy Bay, as often as necessary — as Ramsay explained, "Sandy Bay, a former detachment point, had a resident exMLA, and the possibility of a complaint to the Attorney General's department outweighed the record of violence at Deschambault." A few weeks later, Ramsay received word that two First Nations men in Deschambault had been shot, one of whom died as a result of his injuries. Ramsay expressed his regret at not ignoring his orders, stating "I'll never forget my feelings as I investigated that killing. I couldn't reconcile the fact that I could charter into one village and not the other."

Jack Ramsay, "My Case against the RCMP," *Maclean's*, July 1, 1972, https://archive.macleans.ca/article/1972/7/1/my-case-against-the-rcmp

1978, Quebec

Charles Philion, Superintendent and the Chief Personnel Officer for Quebec, wrote to RCMP Headquarters in 1978 to complain about a manual on recruiting and personnel management that he had discovered. The manual, written for the RCMP in 1944 by Roderick Haig-Brown, a captain in the Canadian army seconded to help establish the RCMP's personnel department, included statements such as "French Canadians are less stable than English Canadians . . . French Canadians are ignorant because of religious and nationalist influences . . . Canadians of central European and Ukrainian backgrounds tend to be violent and unpredictable . . . Germans and Scandinavians have better natural abilities as policemen than many other racial groups . . . Indians on a reserve near Montreal were violent and quick-tempered." Commissioner Robert Simmonds acknowledged that Philion's complaint had merit. Another senior personnel officer stated in a memo that the manual was only referred to "in its historical perspective" but admitted that having it on hand "does raise suspicion that it still influences thinking within the (staffing and personnel) function." The senior officers discussed destroying all evidence of the manual, but eventually decided to send a microfilm copy to the RCMP archives under limited access. Philion wrote again to request that the RCMP condemn the manual, arguing that "the plain outright discrimination which I have personally experienced and witnessed, leads me to believe this document has had more influence than is generally acknowledged." After much discussion, Commissioner Simmonds finally put in writing his "personal displeasure" at the suggestion in the manual that "some particular group or race of Canadian is in any way inferior to another."

Peter Moon, "RCMP Used 'Racist' Manual: Report on Recruiting was Hidden in Archives after 35 Years," *Globe and Mail*, November 3, 1986.

1986, Alberta

Gordon Hum, a Chinese Canadian man born in Halifax, was pulled over for speeding by Constable Jackson Nash in Alberta in 1983. Nash asked Hum where he was born, and requested a birth certificate, prompting Hum to react in anger, calling Nash a "racist pig." Nash arrested Hum and placed him in jail for outstanding parking tickets, which were later discovered to have been paid. Hum made a complaint to the Canadian Human Rights Commission. During the tribunal, Nash argued that he was following standard RCMP practice in requesting proof of citizenship, and Superintendent D.R. Barker testified that "being non-white was enough to trigger a Mountie's suspicion of immigration illegality." Members of the RCMP stated that if two people were acting suspiciously, "the non-white would be asked for proof of citizenship while the white would only be questioned if dress or accent was different." The tribunal found in Hum's favour, awarding him $250 for "injury to his feelings and self-respect," and ordered Commissioner Robert Simmonds "to issue an official directive telling all Mounties to cease the widespread discriminatory practice."

"Arresting Injustice," *Ottawa Citizen*, December 15, 1986.

Matthew Fisher, "Citizenship Queries Violation of Rights, Driver Tells Tribunal," *Globe and Mail*, September 4, 1986.

Peter Calamai, "RCMP Ordered to End Bias against Non-Whites," *Gazette* (Montreal), December 12, 1986.

1990, British Columbia

As a teenager, Baltej Singh Dhillon immigrated to Canada from Malaysia with his family. Through volunteer work as an interpreter for the RCMP, he became interested in policing, and in 1988 formally applied to the RCMP. He met all requirements for entrance, but the RCMP dress code prohibited him from wearing the turban and beard that his Sikh faith obliged him to wear. Dhillon appealed to the Commissioner for changes to the dress code, and the Commissioner recommended the federal government make the changes. This caused controversy both within the RCMP and with the public. The Reform Party campaigned against the change, more than 90,000 Canadians signed a petition and pins were sold mocking the change, containing images of crossed-out turbans and racist caricatures with phrases like "Keep the RCMP Canadian", "Don't Mess with the Dress" and "RCMP Paki." In March 1990, the Mulroney government announced that the changes to the dress code would go through, and Dhillon was able to join and complete his training. Dhillon got death threats in the mail, and retired RCMP members attempted to make legal challenges to the change. The government's decision was confirmed in 1996 by the Canadian Human Rights Commission and the Supreme Court of Canada.

Photocopy of images of pins, in the author's possession.

Richard Foot, "Baltej Dhillon Case," *Canadian Encyclopedia*, November 14, 2016, www.thecanadianencyclopedia.ca/en/article/baltej-dhillon-case.

"The Turban that Rocked the RCMP: How Baltej Singh Dhillon Challenged the RCMP — and Won," *CBC News*, May 11, 2017, www.cbc.ca/2017/canadathestoryofus/the-turban-that-rocked-the-rcmp-how-baltej-singh-dhillon-challenged-the-rcmp-and-won-1.4110271.

1993, British Columbia

Yarinder Singh Brar, a Sikh constable, filed a complaint with the Canadian Human Rights Commission after four years of service in the RCMP over the harassment he experienced from fellow officers and supervisors. Brar said that his complaint was about the "over-all attitude of the RCMP toward minorities. On the one hand, they have this philosophy that they want to hire more minorities, but yet, inside, those views aren't shared by the management or the constable-level personnel." Brar had evidence to support his claims. During a party at his house, he took a video of a sergeant jokingly calling him a "stupid, bald-headed Paki." He had a copy of a calendar he found in his detachment with a Mountie depicted with a turban and dagger with the caption, "Is this Canadian or does this make you Sikh?" He had copies of racist jokes and poems that were posted on bulletin boards in his detachment. Brar noted that his complaints within the RCMP were not acted on, and talking to officers about their behaviour only led to being ostracized. In a 1993 memo from Brar's supervisor, Superintendent Stan Wilcox, to Vancouver RCMP headquarters Wilcox called Brar "unmanageable" and said he is "fast to complain about intimidation and harassment."

Kim Pemberton, "Mountie of Asian Descent Claims Racial Taunts at Hands of Colleagues," *Vancouver Sun*, February 20, 1993.

1993, British Columbia

Davinder Singh Khaper, a Sikh man from Ontario, gave up his beard and turban to join the RCMP in 1989, just a year before Dhillon successfully fought to change the dress code. He was posted to Surrey, BC, in 1990 where he experienced ongoing harassment. He was called "Ghandi" and "Samosa" by other officers during his training, who justified their behaviour by saying "if you can't put up with racial remarks in the office, how are you going to do it on the road?" Khaper went on sick leave in 1991 and in 1992 suffered a nervous breakdown. Shortly afterwards he resigned from the RCMP. Khaper later stated that his "resignation was extracted under undue influence," and filed a complaint with the Canadian Human Rights Commission about the harassment he experienced while working for the RCMP. Khaper stated that "The RCMP treats minority and female officers like second-class citizens. You have to be part of the team. And if you're not, you're blackballed."

Wendy McLellan, "Second Mountie Sues on Slurs: 'They Called Me Ghandi, Samosa,'" *Province* (Vancouver), March 3, 1993.

1994, Nova Scotia

Burnley "Rocky" Jones and his wife Joan were leading activists in Halifax's black community when the Black Panthers came to town in the 1960s. The RCMP had the Joneses, along with almost everyone involved in the civil rights movement in Nova Scotia, under surveillance in the sixties and seventies. The Canadian Press obtained the files related to the surveillance under an Access to Information request. The Joneses recalled their telephone being shut off in the night, and receiving their mail once a week instead of daily like their neighbours. Burnley Jones stated that the RCMP should apologize, calling the documents in the file "some of the most blatantly racist documents that I've seen in the 20th century that come through government." In addition to documents that call black women "prolific child bearers" and black men "layabouts," a 1968 report in the file states that "Negro settlements in Halifax County could become headaches in the space of a few months with the influence of capable radical Negro organizers." A second report from that year by Constable K.J. Good states that though the Black Panther movement is growing, "their disciples consist mainly of the illiterate, semi-illiterate and hoodlums."

Alan Jeffers, "RCMP Spied on Blacks in '60s; Stereotype-Ridden Documents Detail Nova Scotia Operations," *Gazette* (Montreal), April 11, 1994.

Alan Jeffers, "RCMP Spy Files Rife with Racism, Documents Show; Activist Calls for Apology," *Ottawa Citizen*, April 11, 1994.

1995, United States
Beginning in 1980, A retired member of the United States Bureau of Alcohol, Tobacco and Firearms (ATF) held an annual spring event in Tennessee involving a picnic, sports and drinking, called the "Good Old Boys Round-Up." In 1995, RCMP members were reported as attending the whites-only event, which greeted members at the entry with a "Nigger Check Point" and a hand-made sign saying "Any Niggers in the Car?" The RCMP conducted an investigation on the event, and RCMP Sergeant Pierre Patenaude said no member had been sent there by the RCMP, "but if they were there knowing that it was a racist thing, yes, they will face disciplinary action." In 1996, the RCMP confirmed that one member had attended the 1995 event, but since the officer was not on duty no disciplinary action was taken.

"ATF Gets Revenge on the Alabama Militia," *John Burke's Society*, May 3, 2007, http://johnburkessociety.blogspot.com/2007/05/atf-gets-revenge-on-alabama-militia.html.

Bruce Cheadle, "Brass Probes RCMP Role at American Racist Picnic," *Ottawa Citizen*, July 25, 1995.

"Summer Bash by Police Officers a Racist Affair, U.S. Officials Find," *Ottawa Citizen*, March 14, 1996.

1999, Saskatchewan
Ali Tahmourpour, an Iranian Muslim man, completed two-thirds of the RCMP training program in Regina in 1999 before he was suddenly terminated. When he reapplied a few months later, common practice for recruits, he learned of a note in his file indicating that he should not be

reconsidered. Tahmourpour had experienced harassment and discrimination during his time at Depot, including "condescending and hostile" comments from a superior officer about a pendant he wore as a sign of his faith. Tahmourpour's first complaint to the Canadian Human Rights Commission over racial harassment was dismissed in 2003. He fought for years to have his case heard, and finally the Federal Court ordered the CHRC to open a new investigation, including statistics Tahmourpour had received through an Access to Information request that showed a significantly higher attrition rate for visible minorities than other recruits. In 2006, the CHRC ruled that Tahmourpour's case should be heard by a Canadian Human Rights Tribunal. In 2008 Tahmourpour was award $500,000 in damages and lost wages and given the chance to reapply to the RCMP. Tahmourpour intended to continue pursuing a career in the RCMP, and said, "I just hope that after this, the RCMP can again become a national icon that we can be proud of."

Harold Levy, "Former Cadet Wins Right to Hearing," *Toronto Star*, April 18, 2006.

Kirk Makin, "Racial Taunts Cost Mounties $500,000," *Globe and Mail*, April 17, 2008.

Tobi Cohen, "Ex-RCMP Cadet Wins Discrimination Case, Gets Second Shot at Dream of Being a Mountie," *Canadian Press*, April 16, 2008.

2005, Ontario

Dean Fontaine, a recently retired RCMP officer, complained when he received an email at his new workplace, the Assembly of First Nations. It had been forwarded to nearly two dozen people, including RCMP officers, government employees other police officers. The email contained an audio file to a song called the "Native Rap," with lyrics like "The RCMP is always chasing me/'Cause I'm a smelly fucking native and I can't even see." The song goes on to describe "natives robbing liquor stores, punching old ladies, 'curb-stomping Whities,' slapping women and shaking babies." When CBC got a copy of the file, they were able to trace its origin to an officer in the Peel Regional Police. Staff Sergeant Paul Marsh told CBC the RCMP had been investigating the email, and that the RCMP encourages employees to come forward if they experience racial harassment. A number of RCMP officers told CBC that complaining about harassment would "lead to being ostracized by co-workers and can ruin any chance of promotion within the force."

"Racist Email Spurs Probes among RCMP, Police," *CBC News*, November 22, 2005, https://www.cbc.ca/news/canada/racist-e-mail-spurs-probes-among-rcmp-police-1.553375.

2005, British Columbia

In August 2005, Glenn Shuter, a First Nations man, was arrested in Merritt, BC, by Constable Saxon Peters after being accused of stealing a police bicycle. Peters beat Shuter, punching him hard enough to break teeth. After the beating, he drove Shuter ten kilometres out of town and left him to walk home. Shuter would only reluctantly talk to RCMP about this incident. In 2007, the unusual charge of torture was added to the charges Peters was facing (but was later dropped), which included aggravated assault, unlawful confinement and obstruction of justice. Roberta Coutlee, Shuter's sister, said she was glad to see charges laid, but that "There's a lot of racism here. Glenn's not the only one that's been beat." Peters pleaded guilty to the charge of assault causing bodily harm in 2008.

"Meritt RCMP Member Pleads Guilty," *Meritt Herald*, October 14, 2018
"RCMP Officer Charged with Torture," *CBC News*, February 7, 2007, https://www.cbc.ca/news/canada/british-columbia/rcmp-officer-charged-with-torture-1.688344.
Robert Koopmans, "RCMP Officer Charged with Torture," *Province* (Vancouver), February 7, 2007.

2007, Afghanistan

Corporal Greg Blain and Sergeant Derrick Ross, two First Nations RCMP members from BC, were sent to Kandahar as part of Canadian Civilian Policing Contingent to teach policing techniques to Afghan recruits. The policing contingent was split into two groups — Team A was mostly white, while Team B was a multi-ethnic group. Team B was treated as inferior by the white officers, receiving targeted ill treatment and only being given menial tasks despite their skills and experience. The two filed lawsuits based on their experiences, claiming they were "harassed and challenged by the RCMP when they returned to Canada and lost promotions as a result of their complaints." Blain later launched a human rights complaint against the RCMP for years of "demeaning conduct" throughout his career.

Jason Proctor, "Attorney General Seeks to Halt Mountie's Human Rights Hearing," *CBC News*, May 22, 2012.
"RCMP Officers Sue Force, Allege Racism," *CBC News*, September 15, 2009, https://www.cbc.ca/news/canada/british-columbia/rcmp-officers-sue-force-allege-racism-1.858216.

2008, Nova Scotia

Staff Sergeant Wylie Grimm was put on administrative leave in 2005 after making racist and sexual comments to two women working in the detachment over the course of two years. In 2008, Assistant Commissioner Ian Atkins apologized on behalf of the RCMP to the town, and especially the black community in Digby, for Grimm's behaviour. He stated that "we took great efforts to carry out an internal investigation," but were "unable to bring full accountability because of the retirement of the commander." Members of the black community in Digby were quoted saying that "young black males are stopped and questioned by Digby Mounties for no reason, proving systemic racism is still at work in the area." Reverend Alden Fells said that Grimm was "not an island. He couldn't act that way on his own and go undetected that long unless the system accommodated his behaviour."

Brian Medel, "Scandal-Plagued Digby RCMP to Get New Boss," *Yarmouth Bureau*, December 28, 2005.
Brian Medel, "RCMP Apologizes to Digby," *Yarmouth Bureau*, January 30, 2008.
Charles Mandel, "Apology Intended to Help Town Heal," *Canwest News Service*, January 31, 2008.

2011, British Columbia

In 2010, David Eby of the British Columbia Civil Liberties Association (BCCLA) conducted fourteen workshops in rural and northern areas of BC in order to identify systemic problems with the RCMP that should be addressed during the province's ongoing contract negotiations with the RCMP. In Terrace, Eby noted serious issues with racism against First Nations, abuse of authority and police brutality. He recommended that the RCMP and the province investigate the many "drastic . . . unsettling" stories he heard there. The RCMP responded that "we are not just here arresting First Nations or homeless people. It is based on behaviour, not race." Eby recommended that the RCMP move away from investigating its own officers, and that problem officers face harsher punishments. He said, "My impression is the RCMP is a lot like the old Catholic Church around residential schools. A handful of problem officers are being shuffled from detachment to detachment. The RCMP knows full well who they are, and they need to get rid of them."

• "A Few Bad Apples May Be Spoiling Public Confidence in RCMP Detachment in BC's Northern Centres — But the Rot Seems to Have Spread to the Core in Terrace, Says Author of New Report," *Province* (Vancouver), February 9, 2011.

2013, Nova Scotia

Brendan Clarke, a nineteen-year-old African Nova Scotian man, was making a purchase at a corner store in Digby in 2002 with a hundred dollar bill. Though the bill was real, the clerk suspected it might be counterfeit and called police. The video from the store shows RCMP officers coming up to Clarke from behind and punching him in the head as they restrained him. The officers brought Clarke outside where they kicked and pepper-sprayed him before putting him in the back of the RCMP car. Clarke filed a lawsuit, which was settled in 2013 with the RCMP apologizing and paying $248,000.

"Digby Man Gets $248K after Police Assault," *CBC News*, June 17, 2003.

2015, Quebec

RCMP Commissioner Bob Paulson met with chiefs and other delegates from First Nations communities at an annual meeting put together by the Assembly of First Nations. Grand Chief Doug Kelly of the Sto:lo Tribal Council from BC confronted Paulson, saying "We encounter racism every single day. Some of the worst racists carry a gun and they carry a badge authorized by you, Commissioner Paulson, to do the work. We need you to confront racism in the ranks." In a surprising admission, Paulson replied, "I understand that there are racists in my police force. I don't want them to be in my police force." He urged those in attendance to "have confidence in the processes that exist, up to and including calling me if you are having a problem with a racist in your jurisdiction or any other problem." Dawn Lavell-Harvard, president of the Native Women's Association of Canada, thought Paulson's remarks were important to the ongoing crisis of missing and murdered Indigenous women, saying, "If we're going to be able to implement real change . . . to make our women and girls safe, then it has to be a significant part of the inquiry because it is right now a significant part of the problem."

Susana Mas, "Bob Paulson Says He Doesn't Want Racists Inside RCMP Ranks," *CBC News*, December 9, 2015.

INDEX